Let God Arise

LET GOD ARISE!

MAKING WAY FOR REVIVAL

Bob Dunnett

*With a Foreword
by
Colin Urquhart*

HarperCollins

Marshall Pickering

William Collins Sons & Co. Ltd.
London · Glasgow · Sydney · Auckland
Toronto · Johannesburg

First published in Great Britain in 1990 by Marshall
Pickering

Marshall Pickering is an imprint of
Collins Religious Division,
part of the HarperCollins Publishing Group
8 Grafton Street, London W1X 3LA

Typeset by Medcalf Type Ltd., Bicester, Oxon.
Printed and bound in Great Britain by
Cox & Wyman Ltd., Cardiff Road, Reading, Berks.

Contents

Foreword

I once heard a theologian remark that he didn't believe in revivals because they always come to an end! Such attitudes demonstrate the Church's need of revival.

It would be wonderful if churches everywhere ministered continuously in the full power of the Holy Spirit. Unfortunately this is far from the case. Churches need revival and Bob Dunnett's book is timely, for it not only faces the need, but directs the reader to the answer.

For centuries men have been preoccupied with their ecclesiastical structures. Their vision of renewal has been a revival of those structures. Some want an Anglican revival, a Baptist revival, a Catholic revival, a Methodist revival, a Pentecostal revival and so on. Today after only a few years of their existence, people are looking for a revival in their new ''house churches'' or nondenominational fellowships.

God is only interested in a Holy Spirit revival. Bob Dunnett points us to the Acts of the Apostles as being the model God has given to the Church. Whenever revival has been experienced historically in the Church, there has been a revival of the Holy Spirit's power and activity. Principles experienced in apostolic times re-emerge in the life of the Church.

I commend this book because it is biblically based in its perspective and is historically informative. Both challenge us to believing prayer for God to move in powerful ways in our own nation in this generation.

Many of us believe this to be His intention. He has promised such a movement of His Spirit through many prophetic witnesses. This book is a significant contribution to the build-up of such a move of God. It will stimulate the longing, faith and prayers of those who desire to see the Kingdom of God extended for His glory; to see great multitudes of people delivered from the dominion of darkness and made the children of light.

There are many specific features of this book I would like to commend. The emphasis on believing prayer is central to revival. Bob points us to the truth that such prayer is a response to God's Word, His promises, His intentions and His initiative. It is not our idea; it is His! For this reason alone, we can be expectant that God will hear and answer us.

"Revival is the coming of the Spirit in the full flow of His power." There can be no revival apart from the Holy Spirit's activity. Whenever the full impact of the Spirit's presence is experienced, large-scale conversion of unbelievers results. Bob describes this as the crowning glory of revival.

Baptism in the Holy Spirit is an empowering for ministry and will result in such fruit. The biblical analysis of this experience is compelling, and is neglected to the believer's great loss. For he can only be as effective in ministry as he is open to the Holy Spirit's enabling and empowering.

Revivals today, as in the Acts of the Apostles, are attended by signs and wonders which give rise to great evangelistic opportunities. They are not the toys of charismatic meetings, but the means by which Jesus and the apostles made the world sit up and take notice of their message.

Whenever the Spirit moves in freedom, there is a great increase in evangelistic fervour. People are moved with love to face the cost of intercessory prayer for the lost. Anointed preachers are raised up by God. There is a rekindling of missionary zeal.

But above all there is a release of love and compassion among God's people; a longing to made Jesus known; a sharing of resources to see needs met; a greater involvement in social action. God's children demonstrate that God cares.

And because He cares, He answers in loving and powerful ways.

His answer to the cry of our hearts to revive the Church and see the nation evangelised is simple: THE HOLY SPIRIT!

Colin Urquhart

Preface

Look among the nations and watch —
and be utterly amazed.
For I am going to do something in
your days that you would not believe,
even if you were told.

Habakkuk 1:5

This book is the outcome of two clear convictions. The first is that those powerful outpourings of the Spirit which we commonly call "revival" are very much in God's heart and purpose for our generation, and will be increasingly significant in the years that lie ahead of us. The second is that it is of great importance that we understand more clearly the nature of these outpourings in order that we can pray the more effectively for them and prepare to be involved in them without being offended by them.

The first of these convictions arises from the fact that we are living in very exciting days when reports of outpourings of the Spirit of God are being received from many parts of the world. It seems, for example, that no sooner have we begun to attempt to take in the measure of God's workings in Korea than we are faced with the news that something even more startling is happening in China, where it appears that in the aftermath of years of strict communist rule, millions have been turning to Christ. Even whilst we are digesting this, we hear of Billy Graham addressing 90,000 people in Hungary, of whom some 25,000 responded to the call to make a decision for Christ. Reports of powerful moves of God's Spirit continue to come in from many Asian Countries, and Africa and South America afford the same sort of testimonies. The fact is that the winds of God that began to blow across the world with increasing force at the turn of this century have never died down and, indeed, seem rather to be increasing. The numbers of people who have turned to Christ as a result of this can only be measured in millions.

That this century did start with some remarkable outpourings of the Spirit is now beyond doubt. Not only was Britain touched during the first decade (especially in Wales) but what Edwin Orr called "the worldwide awakening of the early twentieth century" also affected all the major Protestant denominations throughout North America, Europe, Australasia and South Africa. More importantly, perhaps, it touched the missionary agencies of those churches. The result of this was rapid growth in the churches of Japan, Korea, India, Africa and South America. Orr notes, for example, that the Edinburgh World Missionary Conference of 1910 recognised that in Africa more progress had been made in the first decade of the twentieth century than had been made throughout all the previous history of mission in that continent.

Yet even those remarkable years have given place to a still greater impact of the Spirit as the century has progressed. Successive waves of revival have increased the membership of the Korean church from some 50,000 at the turn of the century to a figure of 12 million. The phenomenon of the emergence of vast churches there has been paralleled in South America and Africa. Having already witnessed many outpourings so far this century, Africa was still gaining some 16,000 Christians a day as the 1980s dawned. Such has been the result of these continual worldwide outpourings that non-white Christians are now in a majority, and the spiritual centre of gravity has shifted away from the West.

We neglect these powerful works of the Spirit of God in the world throughout this century at our peril. Such neglect cramps our spirit and shrinks our vision of the greatness of God's purposes for His world at this time. If, on the other hand, we carefully measure in our hearts the great works of the Spirit which have produced such a forward movement, we are left with no other desire than that God should continue and extend them through further outpourings. "By my Spirit" becomes more than ever indelibly marked in our hearts as the supreme keynote of all true advances of the work of God.

I do not think any of us will need reminding that there is yet a great deal more ground to be gained for the Kingdom in this world of ours. There are parts which have yet to feel the full measure of an outpouring of the Spirit, and have yet to feel an awakening. There are parts which have become very dry (not least our own country and Europe) and which have not felt the power of a widespread spiritual revival for many a decade. It is for these that the vision of the power and effect of the outpouring of the Spirit must be kept constantly burning.

As to the second conviction, namely the need to understand the nature of spiritual outpourings, it is vital that we have not only historical but also biblical understanding. It is when we see something clearly in Scripture that our vision for it is secured and we gain the confidence and persistence to pray on in faith for it to happen. Moreover, such biblical understanding enables us to pray in more precise terms. A number of excellent attempts in this direction have been published. This present contribution is added in the hope that the biblical insights which I have found most helpful in many years of praying for revival might be of help to others in their praying. While the substance may not differ essentially from that of other books, the approach may, and it is this different approach that I trust might be helpful.

My approach to revival has always been based on the Acts of the Apostles. That book presents us with a picture of the Church moving in the full flood of the outpoured Spirit. It is a picture of what the revived Church can be, or of the kind of things we may expect to happen to the Church (and the world) when revival comes. What we see in Acts may not strictly deserve to be called a revival, for it does not show us a church returning from deadness and dryness (unless that

7

can describe the state of the disciples prior to Pentecost!). But it does undoubtedly show us the kind of thing we are aiming for when we bend our knees to seek for an outpouring of the Spirit. "Revival", someone has remarked, "is a return to Pentecost".

Acts is of tremendous value because it does not exist in an atmosphere of mere promise and imagery, wonderful and instructive though all that is; rather, it represents a factual, "on the ground" description of precisely the kind of things that do happen when the Spirit is poured out. We see the "wilderness blossom as the rose" as thousands accept the Messiah in the very city where he was crucified. We actually see the beautiful "trees of planting" of the Old Testament promise taking shape, for example, in the flesh and blood of powerful evangelists.

For many years I have loved the Old Testament revival promises. I have prayed over them many, many times, and yet always Acts has come back into focus as the essential plan or touchstone of what revival means in practice.

Peter began his first Pentecostal sermon with the words, "This is that . . . " Acts "is that" to which the Old Testament prophetic promises pointed when they spoke of the outpouring of the Spirit. If we are seeking for revival in terms of those promises, we are seeking for a return to what God did in those glorious days of the early Church.

In seeking to understand revival we shall, therefore, be undertaking a thorough examination of crucial aspects of the outpouring of the Spirit as presented to us in Acts. Those aspects all need to become the meat of our prayer for revival. They should guide our requests and stimulate our faith. That is really my reason for writing. I am aware of the tragic fact that the return to Pentecost has in some ways been bitterly contested throughout the century. But the signpost to revival points unmistakably in that direction. I hope the material in this book confirms the rightness of the path which many are already taking and allays the fears of those who are reluctant and apprehensive even yet.

Bob Dunnett

Chapter 1: Open to God

But God has shown me . . .

Acts 10:28

Revival challenges our thinking

If we have a serious concern for revival and long to see it happen, we must be prepared to have our spiritual horizons stretched. For in seeking for revival we are seeking for the Holy Spirit to act in the most powerful of ways. That means we must be prepared for God to take us into experiences which may be unfamiliar to us. If we are not prepared for this, we will not keep pace with the Spirit, and may even find ourselves obstructing Him, no matter how sincere our concern might be. To be unprepared for change is to be unprepared for revival.

Moreover, being ready to keep pace with God means that we may need to be ready for some reinterpretation of our biblical understanding in the light of the new experiences of God that the Spirit might show us. The theology of the past may be powerful and invigorating but it may not always be able to account adequately for the new dimensions which open up as God's purposes unfold in the present.

Let me clarify this statement. I am not speaking here of adding to the God-given revelation that we have in the Bible. It is certainly the case that the Bible contains all that God will ever want to reveal to man, and all that man will ever need to understand about God's dealings with him on this earth. It would, however, be a very unwise, not to say arrogant, man who thought that he had come to a point where God had no surprises for him, and who imagined that

9

his own personal biblical perception was so accurate that it would never need to be amended.

The fact is that while we may well be in possession of a full written revelation of all God's purposes, the degree of our personal apprehension of them could well be lacking at points. An attitude of mind which is open to reorientation of biblical perspective is perfectly consistent with a total acceptance of biblical authority and a readiness to stand for biblical truth. God's Word is unchangeable, but we need to recognise that our understanding of it is at times unlikely to be so well founded.

Failure to appreciate this has been, I believe, one of the greatest obstacles to real progress in the purposes of God. It has certainly been a major obstacle to many when it comes to the Holy Spirit working in revival power. For particularly in the area of revival, God has consistently introduced broader-than-normal horizons of experience and has worked in most unusual ways. Again and again there has been a reluctance to accept them.

This is so important a matter that, before pursuing the major themes underlying the revival blueprint of Acts, we need to pause and examine it in some detail. Before we really earnestly seek God for Holy Spirit blessing we must be ready to adopt this open attitude. It may entail certain dangers, but we need to meet these head-on and not let them deter us in any way. We simply must become people ready to follow the Spirit of God into all the implications of His sovereign activities and manifestations. This is not a call to be gullible, but it is a call to be open.

An apostle challenged

Fortunately, there is a very good biblical treatment of this vital principle which can help us get it clearly into our minds and hearts. As with the other major premises of this book, it comes from the Acts of the Apostles. We find it in chapters 10 and 11, which describe the conversion of Cornelius. The circumstances of this conversion made it a striking event even for revival times. But its theological significance is even more striking. Cornelius was a Gentile, and he was converted, filled with the Holy Spirit and then baptised without being circumcised or associated in any other way with the Jewish race. This has always been recognised as marking a crucial phase in the process by which the Gospel became freed from a narrow Jewish setting, with its traditions of circumcision and the like, and began to be seen as something which the Gentiles could receive simply on the basis of faith. This was a startling development with immense implications for the expansion of the Church, but it came about only because Peter, one of the apostles, was open to God and willing to undergo a change of perspective and a broadening of his spiritual and biblical horizon as the Spirit led him on. It is this openness which we need to study carefully.

The episode began with Peter falling into a trance and seeing a vision as he prayed on a rooftop in Joppa. It was a vision in which God was calling him to kill and eat "unclean" animals, and it was given to him three times. The vision perplexed him, and he was not sure what it meant. Then his prayer time was disturbed by some men calling out for him from below. Precisely at that point the Holy Spirit spoke to Peter and told him that He had sent them and that he must go with them. The callers, who proved to be Gentiles, had brought Peter an invitation from Cornelius, who wished him to go to Caesarea and spend some time in his house there. The meaning of the vision now started to become clear to Peter. God was telling him to go and accept hospitality and food from Gentiles, something he would never have dreamed of doing up to that point. After reaching Caesarea Peter acknowledged as much to Cornelius: "You are well aware that it is against our law for a Jew to associate with a Gentile or visit him. But God has shown me that I should not call any man impure or unclean. So when I was sent for, I came without raising any objection" (Acts 10:28—29). When he heard that Cornelius himself had been visited by an angel, Peter went on to say with even greater

11

emphasis, "I now realise how true it is that God does not show favouritism but accepts men from every nation who fear him and do what is right" (Verse 34).

"I now realise . . ." — that is the key expression in Christian growth! "I can see something I never saw before, something I never imagined could be remotely possible." When hearts are as open as that the Spirit can do His work!

So Peter found himself entering into a Gentile's house and behaving in a manner totally beyond his previous horizon. He was finding it difficult but he was keeping pace with the Spirit. One is reminded of John Wesley's struggles to respond to the promptings he received to preach in the open air — a practice that was totally against his theology and tradition. Initially this way of preaching caused him much pain, but finally he embraced it fully and it was to be vital for the revival work in which he was to be engaged.

However, God was not yet finished. As Peter began to speak to Cornelius about the ministry, death and resurrection of Jesus, the Holy Spirit "came on all who heard the message". God had done a great deal up to this point to break down age-old prejudices, but this direct coming of the Spirit on a Gentile group caused yet more "astonishment" (Acts 10:45). Even the Gentiles had received the Holy Spirit! So Peter now had to take a still larger step in order to keep pace. Here were Gentiles, converted, filled with the Spirit — but uncircumcised! Everybody knew that the Spirit coming onto uncircumcised people was something that just did not happen! Yet Peter was being driven to abandon any thought of requiring Gentiles to undergo Jewish ceremonies. He was coming to realise that God was accepting them just as they were because of their faith. The horizon was getting bigger still. With true spiritual intuition (and great courage), he pressed on and baptised them without circumsising them. The implications for Gentile outreach were to be immense.

Here was a man who was truly open to God, and the outcome was a flood of blessing.

The story does not finish quite at that point.

12

Unfortunately it has a sequel. Such an extraordinary departure from usual traditional behaviour patterns could not pass without a challenge and, once back in Jerusalem, Peter was called to account for his treatment of the Gentiles. Criticism was voiced by a group of believers who were deeply conscious of their Jewish roots and for whom Jewish practices were vital. Both the Old Testament and Jewish traditions were very clear about the position of Gentiles, and Peter had gone too far. Peter's response was very direct. It was not in the least theological or doctrinal. He simply related what the Holy Spirit had done, and concluded, "So if God gave them the same Gift as he gave us . . . who was I to think that I could oppose God?" (Acts 11:17).

Though Acts 11:18 records that these "Judaisers" seemed satisfied with the explanation, we see from 15:1—2 that a substantial group of believers in fact soon reverted to opposition. They began to teach actively and militantly the need for a full return to Jewish rituals.

Thus we meet with a tragic picture of people who, though belonging to God, were not open to God. How frequently this situation has recurred in the history of the Church, and how frequently the work of the Kingdom has been blighted through it! It is not always outsiders who most delay the work of the Kingdom; sometimes it is sincere believers who refuse to allow new light to fall on their dearly held and seemingly biblically based traditions. In order that this problem may be avoided, the principle of being open to God must be clearly (and biblically) spelt out.

Peter at full stretch

We need to examine the details of the story a little more closely in order to get the full import of it. It is instructive to look first at Peter as he himself came to the brink of these new experiences. We need to take careful note of the fact that he was not exactly a "new" Christian! In fact he may well have started his spiritual education as a disciple of John the Baptist. His brother, Andrew, was certainly a disciple

13

of John's, and at the very least Peter was in close touch with all that John was saying and doing (see John 1:35–42).

A greater foundation, of course, was laid whilst he spent his two to three years as a disciple of Jesus Himself. He must have heard Jesus expound again and again the great truths of the Kingdom. He doubtless had the benefit of many personal conversations with Him. He watched Him work miracles of all kinds, and found himself both preaching and healing the sick as his apprenticeship ran its course. He had the benefit of the crucial retrospective Bible studies which Jesus gave to the apostolic band after His resurrection (Acts 1:2). These included "an opening of their minds to understand" the Old Testament prophetic witness to His death and resurrection and, even more important for our purposes, an opening up of their vision to the all-important programme of Gentile outreach (see Luke 24:44–49).

Moreover, all this wealth of understanding and insight came powerfully alive on the Day of Pentecost, when Peter entered into a new dimension of the experience of the Holy Spirit. With great power he preached the resurrection to unbelievers and then taught the secrets of the Kingdom to the ever-increasing crowds. He was, if not the leader of the apostolic band, at least its dominant figure, leading the Church with a powerful preaching, teaching and healing ministry.

Yet this was the man who still had something to learn, some new perspective to appreciate, some old prejudice to discard! He had not reached the end of Jesus warning that "I have much more to say to you, more than you can now bear" (John 16:12). These words still held true. It is not too much to say that even after his years with Jesus and his years of Spirit-filled ministry, he had not grasped in any real sense the might and weight of the great truth that salvation is by grace alone through faith, and that this was true for both Jew and Gentile. A good Reformation theologian might have said of Peter with some accuracy that he had not actually grasped the heart of the Gospel!

Notice the way in which the Spirit led him to appreciate

14

the new dimension. He did not show Peter the truth by revealing it to him through careful doctrinal study and then calling on him to act on such revelation. He chose to confront him with a fact, an experience, a happening to which Peter was driven to adjust. It was an experience which was to reveal to him a crucial theological truth to which he had been blind.

Peter was a man prepared for this, since he was accustomed to the Spirit's methods of vision and direct speaking and was therefore ready for the providential invitation to Cornelius' house. He could step out in faith. Likewise, as a man of the Spirit, he was able to recognise immediately that the coming of the Spirit on the household of Cornelius was a genuine gift of the Spirit, for He came "as He had come at the beginning" (Acts 11:15). This is an all-important factor — an ability to see and recognise a genuine activity of the Holy Spirit, even when it challenges our most deeply held attitudes and our most carefully constructed theology.

Quite obviously, the Spirit could have chosen to reveal these new dimensions to Peter from the pages of Scripture before the events. They were certainly there in the Old Testament. After all, as we shall see more clearly in a moment, Paul was soon to find that the doctrine of Gentile inclusion through faith was thoroughly embedded in the history of Abraham, the founding father of the Jews. Moreover, as the evangelist Matthew was careful to notice, Jesus, in speaking of the true mature of uncleanness to the Pharisees, had taught quite clearly that it was not what went into a man's stomach that defiled him, but rather what came out of his heart. Matthew certainly perceived that this was Jesus' own declaration of the fact that all meats could be considered clean. Peter must have heard this, possibly more than once, but when it came to meeting with Cornelius, the Holy Spirit chose not to recall and enlighten this word of Jesus but instead to give Peter a rather more graphic vision of the same principle and to act in a dramatic fashion. The theological rationale was to come later.

Thus we are faced with the fact that we must be ready for God to choose to lead us into new dimensions in a way which is not in the first instance the product of biblical revelation. The reason why God acts in that sort of way seems reasonably clear: we are frequently so locked up in our own theological perspectives that nothing short of a powerful new experience has any chance of changing them and taking us beyond them.

We have to add immediately, of course, that invariably that new dimension will be clearly seen in the Bible, providing that the experience with which we are presented is not too quickly rejected on a false premise (even a false premise which appears at first sight biblical!).

As far as Peter is concerned the fact of the matter was that until God dealt with him in this Cornelius episode, he was carrying with him something that he had grown up with from boyhood, something that seemed to be so much a part of Scripture and certainly was one of the deepest parts of his Jewish tradition, something that he had never questioned and never expected to question, but which was now to be a hindrance and even a denial of all that the Gospel stood for. In fact, a biblical standpoint he had never thought of questioning had now to be jettisoned.

This is precisely how God still acts, and has to act. For we still carry with us a very great deal of traditional outlook, all too often scripturally supported but ultimately an obstacle to the furtherance of the Gospel and removable only, it seems, by Holy Spirit "confrontation".

It is, of course, quite beside the point to say that Peter did not have the full revelation that we have, and that his was a different case because that revelation was being established. The revelation was in fact already there — he simply had not grasped it!

Working out new experiences biblically

As we have pursued this theme, enough might have been said in passing to indicate that when God does meet with

16

us through direct Holy Spirit revelation and sovereign action this does not mean that we are then loosed from our biblical moorings to float wherever any tide of experience may care to take us. It is important to stress that this is not the case. We may be sure of one thing — if we are being led into genuine Holy Spirit experience and into a broadening of horizons we shall certainly find a biblical warrant and explanation.

It is difficult to say how quickly Peter found the biblical understanding of his experience. He may well have struggled with it for some time. We can, however, watch much more closely the process by which the Apostle Paul reached a firm biblical understanding of the great truth of salvation by faith alone. This also, of course, began with an experience — the confrontation with Jesus on the road to Damascus. Again experience preceded doctrine. But in seeking to understand what had happened to him, Paul began to see much more clearly the nature of God's dealings with rebels such as himself. He saw that it was a process by which God reached out in sheer mercy from his inscrutable will and called men to faith in Jesus. It was a process never of works but always of grace. He had certainly done nothing to merit the forgiveness he received on the Damascus road! It was, he saw, the same process that had always obtained throughout God's dealing with his own people, the Jews. Abraham, the Father of the Jewish nation, had been righteous before God simply because he had believed in what God had promised to do with him. In this way God had accepted him before ever He spoke to him of circumcision. God's promise to Abraham that all nations would be blessed through him had also preceded circumcision and therefore had not been essentially bound up with it. As he scoured the Scriptures it therefore became biblically self-evident to Paul that the Gentiles could come into salvation simply by faith in the offer that God was making to them in Jesus. All this surfaces very obviously both in Romans and Galatians.

How important this biblical rethink and grounding was can be judged by the fact that Paul was able to withstand pressure from opponents of his newfound perspective when they challenged it in Galatia, whereas Peter (and even Barnabas) succumbed and withdrew from eating with Gentiles. This may have something to do with the difference between their personalities, Paul being much stronger, but it may also have to do with the fact that the others had not seen the matter biblically as clearly as Paul had seen it. They had to learn that experiences, no matter how remarkable they may be, frequently do not provide the inner strength required in difficult situations unless thoroughly grounded in biblical truth.

The inevitable opposition

If we can learn a great deal from the Holy Spirit's dealing with Peter over this episode, we can also learn a great deal from the antagonistic reaction that it set up throughout the Church. Unhappily it brings us face to face with something that happens all too frequently in the ongoing life of the Christian community.

The Judaisers took their stance on what seemed to them to be the true biblical tradition and refused to budge from it. They said to Peter accusingly "You went into the house of uncircumcised men and ate with them" (Acts 11:3). That was enough. This attitude distinctly echoes that of the Pharisees when they declared that Jesus could not be of God because he healed on the Sabbath. The rocks of circumcision and the Sabbath belonged to the same order — they must not be moved. The tragic difference, of course, is that the Judaisers were Christians whereas the Pharisees were not. Despite Peter's testimony, they went down to Antioch and told the brothers, "Unless you are circumcised according to the custom taught by Moses you cannot be saved" (Acts 15:12). They also went to Galatia, "throwing the believers into confusion, and trying to pervert the Gospel of Christ" (Galatians 1:7).

It is very important to notice that they were not necessarily a small "off-beat" group, for Paul refers to those who came

18

to Antioch as "certain men who came from James". It seems, then, that even the apostle James was sympathetic to this opinion — at least in the early stages. But to what extent? As one might imagine, the Judaisers had their roots in the Jerusalem church, with its strong Hebraic background. So James, the acknowledged leader of that church, would certainly have felt the full force of their complaints and might well have been swayed by them. It looks very much as though he was not fully persuaded about Peter's viewpoint until some time later, when he heard the combined testimony of Peter, Paul and Barnabas at the Council of Jerusalem (Acts 15:19).

We have, therefore, the picture of one of the leading apostles not being absolutely clear on the issue initially, and actually being implicated in the teaching which was antagonistic to the new God-given dimension. It should never surprise us, therefore, that when in our turn God begins to take us into new experiences and horizons, even some of the most significant leaders within the Church may be slow to accept the new vistas and may even encourage teaching against them. The eventual acceptance by such leaders might well take far longer and be far more grudging than that of James — that is, if it comes at all.

The whole business was, of course, very distressing. When Paul discovered that the Judaising party had had a very significant impact among his Galatian converts, he wrote to them with his own hand (which was not often his practice) and out of a deeply disturbed heart. He could not bear to think that they should turn back to legalism. It was not in Paul's nature to mince words and he roundly said, "If anyone is preaching to you a Gospel other than what you accepted, let him be eternally condemned" (Galatians 1:9). He remonstrated with his converts:"You foolish Galatians! Who has bewitched you?" When episodes like this occur in the Church, when the Holy Spirit is beckoning people on and there is a rejection, it is always distressing. Strong words are said on both sides. Those who hang back tend to accuse those who go on of causing division, and those who go on tend to speak disparagingly of those who do not. Strong words, coming out of genuine love and concern, may well be necessary at times, as Paul evidently felt. At other times the use of such words may not be so loving or so wise.

How absolutely crucial it is that all of us in the Body of Christ should be fully open to the leadings and new dimensions of the Spirit as we move forward with Him. How crucial it is that we should be able to recognise His voice and activity. How devastating it is for us to imagine at any time that we have imbibed everything that He will ever want to reveal to us.

Why did the Judaisers refuse to accept the consequences of the Holy Spirit's activity? Why do people hold back from following hard after new dimensions in the Spirit?

Undoubtedly there is the extraordinary difficulty of having to rethink old and dearly held traditions. The more these have been studied, thought about and actively taught, the more difficult it becomes to relinquish them. It is as though the human personality cannot cope with radical upheaval. And if people are asked to accept the testimony of others, when they themselves (like the Jerusalem party) have not actually been in the middle of the Holy Spirit event personally, the whole thing seems to become too much of a challenge. At that point all too frequently people harden their grip on the very tradition which the Spirit is challenging. Many people find it extremely painful to accept the testimony of experience from others if the implication of that testimony is a demand then they move forward into a spiritual unknown and seriously rethink their traditions.

In this connection it is not without significance that the earliest theological rethink about the old Judaistic patterns in which the early Church was cradled came, not from the Christians converted out of the main, Hebraic, Jerusalem-based stream of Judaism, but from those converted out of its Hellenist stream. The former were deeply tied to the old tradition and its teaching, whereas the latter, being more oriented to the wider Greek world, were more open to new influences and dimensions. It was the Hellenists, notably

Stephen, who first began to hint at the irrelevance of the Temple and certain aspects of the Law of Moses. Stephen was particularly ready to grasp the implications of all that the Holy Spirit was doing in terms of making the old order obsolete (Acts 6:11). We should not be surprised, then, to find that recent converts drawn from a totally non-church background easily and readily move into dimensions of experience which others who are more theologically educated stumble over.

It was this same stream of Hellenist converts whom God used to bring about the Gospel's initial breakout from its confines in Jerusalem. As a result of Stephen's challenge to Judaistic forms, persecution arose against the Church, causing the Christians to scatter and preach right across Palestine and beyond. It was Philip, a Hellenist colleague of Stephen who preached in Samaria (Acts 8:1ff), it was men who had originated from Cyprus and Cyrene who went to Antioch and first preached the Gospel to the Greeks there (Acts 11:20). When those Greeks responded, they were formed into a church and no Judaistic requirements were laid on them. It was Barnabas, a Levite from Cyprus, who authenticated the work which had been done in Antioch when sent there from Jerusalem by the apostles (Acts 11:12ff). These were all men who were open to God, with no overwhelming weight of tradition lying upon them. It was through them that God moved his Kingdom forward, even though their "circumcision" opponents fought bitterly against them.

This survey of the Hellenists and their work should also remind us of the fact that whilst Peter's Cornelius experience was of the greatest importance in establishing new horizons, it was by no means unique. Similar things kept on happening to many others. It is always the case that if the Holy Spirit is trying to take the people of God forward, He will give similar experiences to many people in many places at the same time. The tragedy of the Judaisers was not simply that they rejected one testimony, even if it was the testimony of an apostle, but that they rejected a testimony to the working

21

of the Holy Spirit which was becoming very extensive. This still remains a tragic pattern within the Church.

Paul, in addressing the problem raised by the Judaisers in his Letter to the Galatians, concludes by commenting on what he believed was behind their refusal to accept the witness of the Spirit. It was not just a question of them finding a change of attitude difficult: it was much more a question of them not having the courage to face the consequences of such a change. To accept them would mean ostracism and, even worse, persecution. They were not prepared for that. Paul writes, "Those who want to make a good impression outwardly are trying to compel you to be circumcised. The only reason they do this is to avoid being persecuted for the cross of Christ. . . . they want you to be circumcised that they may boast about your flesh" (Galatians 6:12). In Paul's estimation, leaving a good impression was of greater consequence for these people than following the truth.

Such strictures may seem severe, but they do point to the indisputable fact that fear in some form or another very frequently lies behind a refusal to go on with the Spirit. Often it is the fear of ostracism and misunderstanding that keeps people back from embracing the new dimension. Often it can simply be the fear of something unknown, of something heard about but not yet experienced. It might simply be a fear that is allied to pride, with loss of face too high a price to pay

The call to adjust

The call to seek revival is a call, therefore, to a humble willingness to adjust one's views in accordance with a wise discernment of Holy Spirit activity. We need to be able to discern that the Spirit is at work when His activities are unusual, and obviously revival is a time when this ability is very necessary. Watching the Spirit at work in Acts, and being open to all the possibilities of Holy Spirit activity which such a blueprint depicts for us, would seem to me to be a very important and biblical way of monitoring what we can accept, and so of keeping in step with the Spirit.

The challenge, then, is to come all the way into the book of Acts, to perceive it as a blueprint of God powerfully at work in revival power, to be ready to let it by our guide as we seek after things we have not yet seen, and to let it tutor us in things that stretch both our theology and credulity! If we are going for revival we are going for the Spirit, and if we are going for the Spirit we have got to be ready for the unusual!

Let the church return to Pentecost and
Pentecost will return to her.
Andrew Murray

The antecedents, accompaniments, and
results of revivals are always
substantially the same as in the case of Pentecost.
Charles Finney

Pentecost, is that to be a tradition?..
.. I see no reason why we should not
have a greater Pentecost than Peter
saw. . . .
C. H. Spurgeon

It is generally agreed that the best
way of defining a revival is to say
that it is the church returning to the
books of Acts, that it is a kind of
repetition of Pentecost.
M. Lloyd-Jones

Chapter 2: Divine Blueprint

. . .as at the beginning

Acts 11:15

Thinking biblically about revival

When God leads us into an experience which is beyond our normal horizons, the most important question we can ask is, "Where in the Scriptures can I find an understanding of what is happening to me?" There are, of course, some experiences which are the direct outcome of biblical revelation, and in that situation from the very start we are on solid ground. But frequently we read a book, hear a testimony or actually go through an experience which leaves us happy but perplexed, and then it becomes crucial to seek biblical understanding.

This seeking is crucial on a number of counts. In the first place it enables us to fix clearly the absolute essentials of our experience and distinguish them from non-essentials. In this way we are prevented from getting carried away with things which may merely excite and appeal to the flesh. (Jonathan Edwards' writings on revival, for example, are masterpieces of this kind of distinction.)

In the second place, being able to identify an experience in Scripture brings an assurance of its value and rightness, and enables us to hold on to it when an "evil day" of assaulting doubts comes our way. The Scripture is a necessary and powerful sword against doubts. True spiritual experience is frequently the object of bitter criticism from some quarter or other, and we need a biblical confidence to face such attack.

Thirdly, a true biblical understanding leads us not merely

27

to a more secure grasp of what we have already possessed but may well lead us on to take hold of yet further blessing. Our experience may well be only partial, and a thorough scriptural understanding of it can help to bring it to completion as further possibilities become clear to us.

There is also great additional value in biblical understanding when we are seeking to enter into an experience which others can testify to, but which has not yet been ours. This is particularly important when we are looking at revival. Certainly, for the vast majority of us who are seeking revival in Britain, we are reaching out to something we have yet to experience. It becomes doubly important to inform that search not simply by historical testimony but by biblical understanding. We need a pattern that will guide us accurately and give us confidence in our seeking and praying. Not only do we want to go all the way and secure all that God can give us, but also, when unexpected things happen in answer to our prayers, we do not want to stumble and miss out because we have not been adequately prepared from the Scripture to be ready and open to them.

How then do we understand revival biblically? No matter how much our hearts may have been stirred by reading historical accounts or listening to testimonies, this is the all-important question.

There is a wealth of relevant material in the Old Testament as well as in the New, but I believe our primary model and inspiration is to be found in the Acts of the Apostles. All the great Old Testament revival passages are essentially prophetic pictures pointing to the days when the Spirit would be outpoured. Those prophetic pictures were fulfilled in the outpouring of the Spirit which is so clearly presented to us through the pages of Acts, and they are best seen in relation to that fulfilment. This is in no way to deny those prophetic passages the amazing power and instruction that they still bring. It is simply to put them into their essential New Testament context.

To take Acts as our blueprint seems to me to enable us to avoid any attempt at a simple, one-sentence definition

28

of revival — and such avoidance is surely right. Perhaps there is one definition of that kind that we could attempt, and that is that revival is an outpouring of the Spirit. But even that leaves things indefinite. It has always seemed to me that revival is not something to be defined in a one-sentence concept. Rather, it is a many-sided process of Holy Spirit activity which can only be fully seen in the kind of action panorama that the Book of Acts provides.

Acts is a remarkable description in a short compass of the coming of the Holy Spirit on the disciples at Pentecost and of the consequent and wide expansion of the Church. The narrative starts in Jerusalem and finishes in Rome. In between we see the Spirit moving powerfully on the apostles as they preach and work miracles. We see the Church as an eager witnessing force, and we see the impact of the Spirit on unbelievers. We see enormous growth and the emergence of large churches, and we are made to feel the strength of the opposition that has to be faced. It is a narrative of a Spirit-filled Church, and it has been frequently styled "the Acts of the Holy Spirit".

Acts does not give us, therefore, a theological, doctrinal definition of revival. It actually gives us something which in a sense is very much more edifying. It gives us a living history of a revival. In this respect it is utterly one with the way in which God time and time again speaks to us through the history of His people as told in the Bible. And then, of course, that history is not without its theology!

Historic testimony to the Acts blueprint

A look at the literature that has grown up around successive revivals over the last three centuries shows how frequently those who have been involved in the outpourings of the Spirit have been drawn to this same book of Acts. This literature started to gain its modern momentum in the early eighteenth-century revivals, particularly the so-called Great Awakening in the American Colonies and the outpouring of the Spirit among the Moravians. Right from the start there has been a natural and almost inevitable tendency amongst those who have been involved in awakenings to see their experiences as a reflection of those of the early Church. Acts has had a long and distinguished pedigree as a blueprint of revival, therefore, and it is important that we take due note of this fact. There has been a constant and clear echoing of Peter's own remark at Pentecost that "this [a present revival] is that [the experiences of Acts]". Reflecting on the persistent nature of this testimony helps immensely to make us secure in the biblical vision of revival which we derive from the pages of Acts.

As early as 1736, at the time of that first Great Awakening in America, when "out of a population of 250,000 at least 50,000 were added to the church", a contemporary observer of those events wrote: "The apostolic times seem to have returned upon us: such a display has there been of the power and grace of the divine Spirit in the assemblies of the people, and such testimonies has He given to the work of the Gospel."[1] He realised the great significance of what God was doing and thought it important that accounts of experiences of the Spirit's working should be compiled. He appealed to his readers for such testimonies, saying, "This . . . would be for the honour of the Holy Spirit . . . I cannot but think it would be one of the most useful pieces of church history the people of God are blest with. Perhaps it would come the nearest to the Acts of the Apostles as any thing extant."[2]

The same thinking was present about a century later at the time of the great revival of 1859—60 in Britain. During those days at least a million people in the United Kingdom were converted. Doctor John Weir wrote an account of the impact of that revival on his own province of Ulster in Ireland. As a pastor he personally witnessed many of the extraordinary scenes that took place at that time, and he wrote while the fires of that outbreak were still hot. Yet his words also reveal the deliberate and reflective mood of one who was seeking to make an accurate assessment of these events. Early in the book he drew a careful comparison between what he had witnessed in Ulster and the outpouring of the Spirit in the early Church. He felt it was perfectly accurate to say that "the New Testament dispensation was ushered in by a Revival, by a mighty Awakening, by a glorious outburst of spiritual life". Even more pointedly, he wrote: "Here then [in the Acts] we have the conditions, and here also the primitive and apostolic type and model of a genuine Revival."[3]

He went on to list a number of clear parallels between the apostolic age and the revival experience he had known personally. He felt that Ulster was in the midst of a series of revivals, and he made careful note of the fact that "the apostolic age . . . was marked and rendered ever more memorable and glorious by a series of mighty awakenings."[4] He concluded by reiterating his firm conviction that "we are warranted to expect that what took place in apostolic times, and in connection with the first successes of Christianity, shall again and again be realised in the history of the Church; and this by periodic, special and abundant visitations of heavenly influence."[5] Weir's concluding statement was both brave and forward-looking. As we shall see later, on the whole the Church at that time was not given to looking back to Pentecost for a vision for the future.

Another observer of the 1859 revival, this time in Wales, was the Rev D. Charles, Principal of Trevecca College (itself a product of a previous revival). He witnessed an extraordinary visitation of God's Spirit upon the college and its students, in which there was a great melting of hearts, and a powerful sense of the living presence of God. There is almost an inevitability about the words with which he described this: "Such was the divine influence felt, that the place seemed to be filled with the special presence of God, which gave rise to the suggestion in my mind, 'something like this must Pentecost have been'."[6]

Shortly before these revivals of 1859, George Smeaton, Professor of Exegetics at the Free Church College, Edinburgh ("perhaps the best learned theologian in the

College''), wrote: ''The importance of the book of Acts as the historic narrative of the public effusion of the Holy Spirit cannot be over-estimated. It shows how the first disciples received the ascension gifts, and went forth equipped with them to found the Christian Church.''[7] James Buchanan, Professor of Systematic Theology at Edinburgh, referring to the Acts, wrote: '' . . . in the New Testament we read the authentic account of the most remarkable revival of true religion that has ever occurred in the history of the world.''[8] He went on to argue for the rightness of expecting similar outpourings, and exhorted his readers to draw great courage from the apostolic pages for the task of preaching the Gospel to all the world.

These two theologians were reflecting in these statements an outlook that had been present in Puritan thought some two centuries previously. This outlook (the ''Puritan Hope'') is summed up by Iain Murray in these words: ''the Kingdom of Christ would spread and triumph through the powerful operations of the Holy Spirit poured out upon the Church in revivals . . . New Pentecosts would show Him still to be Lord and Christ.''[9]

Andrew Murray and Samuel Chadwick, two great Christian leaders at the turn of the century, the former a spiritual giant whose books still speak, and the latter a great college principal and evangelist, each wrote a book on Pentecost. These books could be said to deal more with the writers' own personal revivals that with revival movements in general, but the testimony of each writer was the same and pertinent to our theme. It was a return to the Holy Spirit and Pentecost that gave them the key to their personal renewal. These two are mentioned not simply for their own sake but also as examples of the many powerful men of their generation who thought like them.

Elsewhere Andrew Murray, speaking more of the Church in general, wrote:

Even when she strives to accept her calling, to witness to her Lord to the ends of the earth, she does it too little in the faith of the Pentecostal Spirit, and the possession of His Mighty Power. Instead of regarding Pentecost as sunrise she too often speaks and acts as if it had been noonday, from which the light must needs begin to wane. Let the Church return to Pentecost and Pentecost will return to her.[10]

The nineteenth-century writer Albert Barnes, whose great commentary on the Bible ran into many editions, wrote: "the day which shall convince the great body of professing Christians of the reality and desirableness of revivals will constitute a new era in the history of religion and will precede manifestations of power like that of Pentecost."[11]

Writing in 1927, the historian John Greenfield looked back at the great revival which had broken out exactly two hundred years earlier in Herrnhutt in Moravia, and which had had an astonishing effect both in Europe and America. He saw that event as a return to Pentecost, and quoted a fellow Moravian historian who viewed it in a similar fashion:

There is nothing in the New Testament to indicate that Pentecost was to be the one and only fulfilment of this promise [of the outpouring of the Spirit]. On the contrary we read in the book of Acts of many outpourings. Church History abounds in records of special outpourings, and verily the 13th of August 1727 was a day of the outpouring of the Holy Spirit.[12]

The ministry of Rees Howell provides an interesting example of the connection between revival and the book of Acts. He received great blessing from the Welsh revival, and in later years, whilst doing missionary work in Portuguese East Africa, spoke to the Africans about that revival and said that God could do among them what he had done in Wales. Norman Grubb writes, "they asked him to preach about it, of course by interpretation. They had no word in their language for revival, so he told them about Pentecost."[13] A mighty revival then followed!

Thus reflection on the revivals that happened over the years up to the early part of this century led to an increasingly clear grasp of the truth that in a very real sense they were manifestations of the Holy Spirit of the same order as those which had been witnessed in the earliest days of Christianity. Revival was a return to Acts: to be able to see it like that was to understand it and feel the spirit of it.

Some recent thinking

The preaching and writing of those who have more recently studied and worked for revivals strongly confirms this outlook. Speaking at Westminster Chapel during a year-long series of sermons on revival, Martyn Lloyd-Jones said: " . . .every time you get one of these great and glorious, and mighty periods of (revival) you will find that in every instance, it seems to be a returning to something that had obtained before. Indeed I will go further — you will find that every one of them seems to be a returning to what you can read in the Acts of the Apostles."[14] He graphically described Isaac returning to the old wells which his father had dug and finding fresh water again. Revival is a return to the old well — to Pentecost.

Lloyd-Jones remained very insistent on this matter, and for sheer clarity it is worth quoting from the address which he gave at the Westminster Conference in the year of his revival sermons (1959). He said:

What we read about the church in the New Testament is an account of revival. . . . When you read the history of revivals, are you at once reminded of the book of Acts of the Apostles? The church always looks like the church in the New Testament when she is in the midst of revival. The New Testament was a period of revival'; the great outpouring on the day of Pentecost was continued.[15]

For some fifty years Dr Edwin Orr made the study of revivals his all-consuming occupation, researching on the widest possible front. It is from him that perhaps the most definitive statements of the connection between the early days of the Church and revivals have come. He affirmed:

> The major marks of an evangelical awakening are always some repetition of the phenomena of the Acts of the Apostles. . . . The events recorded in Acts have been repeated in full or lesser degree in the Awakenings of the past centuries. . . . It is more than interesting to compare the characteristics of the Awakenings of various decades with the prototype of evangelical revivals in the Acts of the Apostles, a perennial textbook for such movements.[16]

Thus for him "the patterns and progress" of revivals are thoroughly anticipated in the apostolic outpouring.

All this amply shows that there has been a long and very distinguished line of opinion which has viewed Pentecost as a model of revival to be embraced and sought after. This was the case well before the emergence of the Pentecostal groupings at the beginning of this century, of course. In the lives and hearts of these men the return to Pentecost was all-important. Pentecost was intimately tied up with revival, and Pentecost was not a denominational issue. It is a very great pity indeed that it ever became one. We may agree entirely with Peter Lewis' assertion in his foreword to *Joy Unspeakable* by Martyn Lloyd-Jones that "Acts chapter 2 and the ensuing history of the apostolic church is more than charismatic experience and doctrinal insight. It is revival in archetypal form."

The fact of the matter is that in the ongoing life of the Church there has been an increasing manifestation of experiences that have driven people back to Acts as the only place where they can find any comprehensive description and understanding of such experiences. The tremendous "baptisms of power" of a Charles Finney, the extraordinary waves of conviction of sin which Wesley witnessed among miners, and Brainherd witnessed among North American

Indians, the great flow of Jesus-centred praise from the Moravians — time and again these were the hallmarks of movements of revival, and they opened the pages of Acts afresh. Out own century has seen not merely these experiences, but also a whole host of others, as God has poured out his Spirit across the world. Ours has been a century of amazing revelation of the power of God, of repetition of all the aspects of his mighty working which were witnessed in those early apostolic days. We have been privileged to see everything from immense conviction of sin to mighty preaching with sign and wonder, all leading to vast numbers of people being won for the Kingdom.

Opposition to the testimony of Acts

One would have thought that there would have been an eager, all-round acceptance of the rediscovery of the pattern of the apostolic Church, and that there would have been a recognition and an applauding of such an emergence of Holy Spirit activity. Sadly, that has not been the case. There has been a strange reluctance in many quarters to return to all that Pentecost implies. Sometimes there has even been bitter opposition to such a return. The challenge of Acts has, therefore, been fenced off by a number of theological walls rather than accepted and sought after.

For example, despite all that God was doing in powerful awakenings, the middle years of the nineteenth century saw the emergence of a very rigid attitude in which even the very idea of seeking God for the Holy Spirit was considered to be thoroughly unbiblical. There was an insistence that because Christians already had the Holy Spirit they could assume Pentecost. Equally dogmatically, it was asserted that it was not within the mind and will of God to repeat in our days the extraordinary happenings of those early days. It was insisted that any phenomena which remotely resembled such happenings could not be of God. Sign and wonder, healing and spiritual gifts had no part in modern Holy Spirit activity. If they betokened anything, it was the presence of the devil.

The real tragedy of this quite widespread and influential attitude (and it is still with us) was that it came from Bible-loving Christians. Yet it prevented the people of God from seeking Him for the new dimensions that He had already begun to manifest, and it blinded people to the real nature and significance of those dimensions, even though they grew stronger and became more clearly authenticated in the experience of growing numbers of Christian people. It certainly blocked any serious vision for revival amongst those who adopted it.

Such attitudes were, however, strongly resisted from the start by those who were moving in the full flood of spiritual revival. During one of his last sermons D. L. Moody, the great nineteenth-century evangelist, put his finger on this outlook and pointedly challenged it:

See how He (the Spirit) came on the day of Pentecost! It is not carnal to pray that He may come again and that the place may be shaken. I believe Pentecost was but a specimen day. I think the church has made this woeful mistake that Pentecost was a miracle never to be repeated. I have thought, too, that Pentecost was a miracle that was not to be repeated. I believe now that if we looked on Pentecost as a specimen day and began to pray, we should have the old Pentecostal fire here in Boston.

A good deal more recently (1958), Arthur Skevington Wood wrote these words:

The story of Acts Two is widely known amongst Christian people but sadly misunderstood. It is wrongly regarded as an isolated occasion. In one sense, of course, the events of the first Whitsuntide were unique and incapable of repetition. The initial effusion of the Holy Spirit marked a distinct epoch in sacred history. There can never again be an original gift of the Spirit to the Church. But the error into which so many believers fall is the supposition that the experience of Pentecost cannot be renewed in succeeding generations. The consequence is that the idea of revival recedes from view. An elementary acquaintance with church history would dispel such a regrettable and indeed tragic misconception. It would reveal beyond denial that God from time to time refreshed His heritage with outpourings of the Spirit almost as remarkable as Pentecost.[17]

He added, "revival is to be measured by the standard of God's inexhaustible power. It may be expected to reach Pentecostal proportions."[18]

Martyn Lloyd-Jones was, characteristically, very definite on this point. Addressing a Westminster Conference, he said:

No more mischievous and misleading theory could be propounded, nor any more dishonouring to the Holy Spirit, than the principle . . . that because the Spirit was poured out at Pentecost, the church has no need, and no warrant, to pray any more for the effusion of the Spirit of God. On the contrary, the more the church asks for the Spirit and waits for His communication, the more she receives.[19]

To state categorically that God does not wish to restore all that belonged to Pentecost is, of course, absolutely without foundation: there is not one piece of scriptural evidence for such an assertion. To go on maintaining it despite all the widespread experience of Pentecostal power and to refuse to come to terms with such experience is very damaging to the real work of the Spirit. The matter is admirably summed up by A. W. Tozer:

A disinterested observer, reading without the handicap of doctrinal prejudice, would surely gather from the scriptures that God desires to advance his work among men by frequent outpourings of the Holy Spirit upon His people as they need them and are prepared to receive them. [Some say that] the Holy Spirit was poured out once for all at Pentecost and has not left the church since. To pray for the Holy Spirit now is to ignore the historical fact of Pentecost. This is the argument used to discourage expectation, and it has been successful in damping down the fervour of many a congregation and silencing their prayers. [It] is contrary to the Word of God and out of harmony with the operations of God in church history.[20]

In more recent years we have been warned by John Stott that "What is *described* in Scripture as having happened to others is not necessarily intended for us" and that "we need to be careful about what we build on the purely descriptive passages of Acts."[21] There is a certain element of truth in this contention. What cannot be accepted, however, is that this sort of view should be pressed so far as to discourage people from entering into the full flow of all the activity of the Holy Spirit as it is portrayed for us by the Spirit Himself in Acts. Much less must such a view be used as justification for not seeking or accepting the powerful waves of spiritual activity which were loosed in Acts. If this view implies that we can comfortably forget the possibility of speaking in tongues or witnessing great crowds of people listening to the preaching of the Gospel, then it is to be rejected. The Book of Acts is a deliberately descriptive piece of writing, given to us in the wisdom of God and intended without question not merely as a piece of antiquarian history but as a stimulus to vision and desire for similar mighty workings of the Spirit. "All Scripture is profitable for doctrine" is God's verdict on Acts, and it must remain ours, too.

A more pertinent criticism of Acts is that which suggest that it is only a partial model of revival.[22] It is often reckoned that before revival can come to the Church as we know it, some degree of restoration in basic discipleship and doctrine must emerge — there must be a return to thorough biblical teaching and so forth. It is pointed out that in the nature of the case, Acts does not demonstrate such a return, and that the reformations depicted in the Old Testament, such as that of Josiah, are an essential additional perspective.

There is no doubt that such Old Testament reformations provide valuable perspectives, and they do demonstrate to us the fact that the rediscovery of vital, long-forgotten truths is of fundamental importance for revival. It was certainly the case that Wesley had to discover afresh the great reformation truth of "salvation by faith alone" before he became one of the great revival leaders of his age. Moreover, he was by no means the only one in the history of revivals whose doctrine and experience needed such reformation. Such pilgrimages are not entirely absent from Acts however. We are introduced to the struggles and revelations of Paul and to the amazing biblical reorientation he needed concerning Jesus. Furthermore, in the first chapter of Acts we are presented with a very clear picture of the kind of assembly of people through whom revival can come. There is no question of the fact that Acts reveals that those people had a very deep personal commitment to a resurrected Jesus, who had been crucified for them and through whom they now had peace with God. Jesus had spent much time bringing about the personal reformation of those one hundred and twenty, leading them through their doubts and misunderstandings so that they were ready to preach the truth. He knew only too well how much depended on their thorough grasp of what He had taught them.

In the light of all this we should, then, feel perfectly confident to move into the pages of Acts and to begin to explore in detail the picture of the revival outpourings of the Holy Spirit which it presents to us. It is, in a very special way, a part of Scripture which has been given to us to help us in our contemporary revival experiences. There is no question that it is meant to clarify and to stimulate. It is the place where we shall find understanding of what God has been doing in the world through revival, where we shall find guidance on what He yet intends to do, and where we shall find direction on how to move with Him in the accomplishment of those purposes.

We shall find that Acts presents us with a call to seek an even greater realisation of Holy Spirit experience in the life of the Church. It will call us to build on all that God has done over many years to bring His people back to those apostolic days. This will not be a call to any particular denominational allegiance, but to a full, biblical experience of the outpoured Holy Spirit.

Notes

1. William Cooper in his Preface to Jonathan Edwards' pamphlet, *Distinguishing Marks of a Work of the Spirit of God*. See *Jonathan Edwards on Revival* (Banner of Truth), p. 77.
2. *Jonathan Edwards on Revival*, p. 85.
3. John Weir, *Heaven Came Down*, p. 5.
4. Ibid., p. 6.
5. Ibid., p. 7.
6. Thomas Phillips, *The Welsh Revival*, p. 14.
7. George Smeaton, *The Doctrine of the Holy Spirit*, p. 47.
8. James Buchanan, *The Office and Work of the Holy Spirit*, p. 47.
9. Iain Murray, *The Puritan Hope*, p. 51.
10. Andrew Murray, *The Spirit of Christ*, p. 105.
11. Quoted by Martyn Lloyd-Jones in his *Revival*, p. 93.
12. J. Greenfield, *Power From On High*, p. 10.
13. N. Grubb, *Rees Howells*, p. 165.
14. Martyn Lloyd-Jones, *Revival*, op. cit., p. 28.
15. Martyn Lloyd-Jones, *The Puritans*, p. 12.
16. Edwin Orr, Introduction to *Evangelical Awakenings in Latin America*.
17. A. Skevington Wood, *Baptism With Fire*, p. 15.
18. Ibid., p. 15.
19. Martyn Lloyd-Jones, *The Puritans*, op. cit.
20. A. W. Tozer, *Paths to Power*, p. 46.
21. J. R. W. Stott, *Baptism and Fullness*, p. 15. See also D. Pawson for a rejoinder in *Normal Christian Birth*, pp. 13–14.
22. R. Lovelace, *Dynamics of Spiritual Life*, p.52. For further

appraisal see M. Lloyd-Jones, *The Puritans*, op., cit., p. 14ff. Lloyd-Jones succinctly sums up the issue: 'If you truly believe in the sovereignty of God, you must believe that, whatever the state of the Church, God can send revival. As a sheer matter of fact that is what God did in the eighteenth century" (p. 15). In other words, a prior return to reformed doctrine is not essential.

Chapter 3: Dark Backcloth

As for what you see here, the time will come when not one stone (of the Temple) will be left on another.

Luke 21:6

Go, stand in the Temple courts . . . and tell the people the full message of this new life.

Acts 5:20

A word of judgement

With Acts in front of us as a guide to revival, one of the first questions we need to pose is, "When can we expect revivals to happen?" We could expand the question and relate it a little more definitely to our own times by asking, "When we look at what is happening around us, isn't it much more likely that we should expect judgement rather than revival?" Or we could put it like this: "What part does repentance, national and personal, play in revival's coming?" These are questions which are inevitably and rightly raised whenever revival is mentioned.

I believe that the apostolic account throws a great deal of light on these issues. We can approach them by simply asking ourselves what was the social and spiritual context in which this first great outpouring of the Holy Spirit was given

A good starting point for an answer to this can be found in Luke 19:41. There we have recorded for us a very poignant scene which took place only a few days before Jesus was crucified. Jesus was on the Mount of Olives gazing at Jerusalem and weeping over it. Out of the tears came a clear prophetic word addressed to the city:

43

As he approached Jerusalem and saw the city, he wept over it and said, "If you, even you, had only known on this day what would bring you peace — but now it is hidden from your eyes. The days will come upon you when your enemies will build an embankment against you and encircle you and hem you in on every side. They will dash you to the ground, you and the children within your walls. They will not leave one stone on another, because you did not recognise the time of God's coming to you."

What devastating words! They placed the whole city under appalling judgement. They are the sort of words which some would rather not accept as coming from the lips of Jesus. But they remain there, quite clear and unavoidable. He prophesied complete destruction.

Moreover, this was not an isolated word. It was a word that was very much in His heart and mind during that last week. It was one which He reiterated, at times in much greater detail. For instance, responding to some remarks made by His disciples about the beauty of the Temple in Jerusalem He said: "As for what you see here, the time will come when not one stone will be left on another; every one of them will be thrown down" (Luke 21:6). For a Temple that had been under construction for several decades and which was the glory of the city, this was a shocking prediction. But Jesus elaborated it, going on to say: "When you see Jerusalem being surrounded by armies, you will know that its desolation is near. . . . there will be great distress in the land and wrath against this people. They will fall by the sword and will be taken as prisoners to all the nations. Jerusalem will be trampled on by the Gentiles." In referring again to the horror which even families would endure in the midst of such judgement, He said, "How dreadful it will be in those days for pregnant women and nursing mothers."

Let us say straight away, therefore, that this word of judgement is the essential dark backcloth to the Pentecostal outpouring of the Spirit. However, before looking more carefully at this word's relevance to the apostolic revival, we need to make a number of general observations on the nature of God's judgements.

The characteristics of God's judgement

First, the tears of Jesus as he wept over the city seem to me to be part of the very spirit of the pronunciation of the judgement. They are not a human reaction to a hard, unfeeling judgement pronounced censoriously by God. The tears are the human expression of the heart of God. His heart weeps even whilst He pronounces His judgements. Judgement is never a happy activity of God. His heart is much more for saving than for judging. We need that same kind of heart whenever we speak of judgements — a heart that weeps for the lost.

Second, despite the aching of God's heart, His judgement is devastating and real. The judgement which Jesus foretold was to come in the form of military oppression. The city was to be literally torn apart. Children would be affected as much as adults. Both would be horribly caught up in the holocaust. The appalling facts of the destruction of Jerusalem in AD 70 are only too well chronicled. It was a precise fulfilment of Jesus' words. The trouble began with a Jewish nationalistic revolt against the Romans. It ended with a gruesome siege of the city, during which the starving Jews even ate human flesh. When they eventually took the city the Romans slaughtered thousands of Jews. It was no ordinary slaughter: significantly, it was a mass crucifixion. The hills around Jerusalem were covered with crucified Jews, until little or no wood was left for any more crosses. God's judgements are terrifying facts.

Third, there is an awful inevitability about the judgement of God. It is easy to sweep aside the warnings of God, as did the Scribes and Pharisees, but not the judgements of which they speak. It is important to notice that the Jewish rulers were warned by Jesus. This was especially so during those last few days before the Crucifixion. His parables left them in no doubt as to what would happen to them if they sought to destroy Him. God does seek to warn nations, but their leaders — those who exercise political power — tend to give scant credence to the spiritual dimension. Their scepticism proves to be no match, however, for the inevitable fulfilment of the word of God.

Fourth, God does not "hurry" His judgements. "The days will come" was the pronouncement of Jesus, and it was a full forty years before those days arrived. In fact it was really the next generation that experienced those devastating days in which the Romans destroyed Jerusalem and fulfilled the prophetic word. This is a very important dimension that we need to keep in mind when we consider judgement — a later generation can actually pay the full price for the sin of a previous generation. There is much in the Scripture that vindicates only too clearly God's warning that the sins of the fathers will be visited on the children. It is much more sensible to recognise the terrible truth of this and act accordingly than to try to quarrel with God over the issue. If children suffer, it is not something to lay at God's door; rather, the blame belongs to "the fathers" whose disobedience was the root cause of the children's suffering. That this happens is only too clearly the case. The younger generation does often suffer for and with the older!

Fifth, the whole city was brought under judgement. Though God deals with individuals, He also deals with groupings of people, indeed with nations. The nation that wilfully and persistently sins is under the same sort of judgement as the individual who sins. There comes a time when whole communities, cities and nations feel the wrath of God.

Finally, the reason for the impending judgement is made very clear by Jesus. It is this: "you did not recognise the time of God's coming to you" (Luke 19:44). This is brought out graphically in the parables addressed to the Jewish rulers during the week before the Crucifixion. In the Parable of the Tenants (Luke 20:8ff) Jesus spoke of the Son who was sent by the Owner of the vineyard to look for fruit. But the tenants killed the Son. As a result the Owner would "come and kill those tenants and give the vineyard to others". Just as surely as Jesus cursed the fig tree which had not produced fruit, so God would curse the nation which instead of showing the fruit of righteousness was prepared to kill its Messiah (Matthew 21:18ff).

Thus the city that would allow its innocent Messiah to be crucified by its religious leaders out of envy and malice, and would turn its back on all the mighty works and authenticated preaching and teaching of the Son of Man, must now pay the inevitable price. It had utterly denied its spiritual birthright and inheritance, and for that there could be only one outcome – judgement.

The mercy that precedes judgement

Despite this inevitable outcome, the extraordinary fact is that within less than two months of the crucifixion of Jesus and the utterance of this word of judgement, God was visiting that great city of Jerusalem, not with judgement but with a tremendous outpouring of the Holy Spirit. The very Temple which was doomed to be razed to the ground became the centre of the most amazing scenes of outpoured mercy. Thousands of people thronged the great and magnificent Portico of Solomon within the Temple, not to hear the Rabbis, but to listen to and to respond to the preaching of the Gospel. They came again and again, eager to hear the apostles teaching the truths of the Kingdom of God. People were mightily healed in and around the Temple's confines. The whole city stood in awe of the presence of God, and the authorities were at a loss to know what to do.

What a mighty demonstration this is of the nature of God working in revival. It is a most eloquent enactment of the truth that God does "in wrath remember mercy". For, even now, while the stage was being prepared for the city's destruction, the love and mercy of God was yet at work, seeking to bring salvation even to those on whom judgement had been pronounced.

If, then, the generation and the people of the city which crucified the Son of God Himself were the objects of divine love poured out through the preaching of the Gospel in revival power, there is tremendous hope for all kinds of situations, no matter how irreversible they may at first appear. There seems to be no limit either in time or place to the extent of God's mercy.

It is important to notice that this outpouring of the Spirit was not in any sense conditional upon the rulers or chief priests repenting of the evil they had done. Had that been required, the door would certainly have been closed to revival blessing for ever. There was no softening of heart among them prior to Pentecost. Indeed, even after the great Pentecostal demonstrations of God's power through the apostles, the leaders of the nation remained as adamantly opposed to the growing Church as they had been to Jesus Himself.

If the outpouring of the Spirit was due to anything, it was due not to rulers who repented but to a group who believed in the promises of God and aligned themselves to His purposes, as we shall see in later chapters. It was the small group who beat their breasts over what had been done at Calvary to whom God looked in order to pour out His blessing.

It is interesting, none the less, to consider what might have been the outcome if the High Priests and Pharisees had repented. What would have been the result if, like the King of Nineveh on hearing the message of Jonah, they had donned sackcloth and called for, or even decreed, a day of humiliation and fasting? I think we have to say that the outworking of judgement might have been very different. God is consistent, and a city in a state of humble repentance, no matter what it has done, is in a place where it can receive forgiveness and, at the very least, a mitigation of judgement. The accounts of the year AD 70 in Jewish history books might have been very different had there been this kind of repentance. There may well have been both national deliverance as well as national revival.

48

However, national repentance, decreed and led by those in authority, is not a common thing either in the biblical record or in Christian history. That does not mean, of course, that we should totally discount it as a possibility and write it off. It may well be a legitimate aiming-point for prayer and action. It must certainly be of enormous consequence whenever it does take place. The seeking of days of national humiliation can only be a laudable objective, and will inevitably be the longing of earnest hearts. Days of National Prayer such as those which took place in Britain during World War II are not impossible. We should not be surprised, however, if political authorities react strongly against moral strictures and calls to repent, or treat them with aloofness and disdain. Unfortunately they have much to lose by admitting the existence of a crisis!

We need to be clear also that, irrespective of any response from rulers when challenged by calls for repentance, we have a constant and prime duty to pray for them, and for whatever legislation they propose, so that peace and righteousness may prevail (1 Timothy 2:1–2).

National repentance, therefore, highly desirable though it is, is not a necessary prelude to God moving in revival power in a nation. That much, at least, is shown by the apostolic account, and it is borne out very clearly in history. For example, the recent tremendous revivals in China have emerged in the presence of a cruel, anti-God regime. Revival is a demonstration of the mercy of God flowing in the midst of his judgements. Through it thousands at least escape eternal judgement as they are brought individually to repentance and faith. This certainly seems to be the normal pattern of revivals in history.

This is completely in accord with all that we know of the essential basis of the way in which God works out salvation for human beings. There has never been any other principle than that encompassed in the words, "God made us alive . . . even when we were dead in transgressions — it is by grace you have been saved" (Ephesians 2:4–5). If revival reflects anything it reflects the sovereign grace and mercy of God being brought to bear upon humanity, even when that humanity is totally unworthy of anything but the most stringent of judgements. God pours out His mercy and His love upon the undeserving, just as Christ died for the undeserving. That is the bottom line of revival.

We can see also from the account in Acts that a great outpouring of the Spirit is not something that inevitably produces a change of heart in the leadership of a nation or a city. In Jerusalem it led initially to bitter persecution by the authorities, and even when that subsided to some extent, deep antagonism remained, as Paul's career only too clearly reveals. Revivals may certainly leaven the lump of society, as we shall see in a later chapter, but they do not necessarily produce the kind of national repentance that might stave off judgements.

What all this means is simply that the outpouring of Holy Spirit blessing can, and does, run either close to or even concurrently with the outpouring of judgement. God does come in mercy, even in the midst of His judgements. There is no warrant for looking for things to improve in order that the Spirit may be outpoured: there is every warrant to hope for a move of grace when things are at their lowest ebb.

Judgement and mercy — the testimony of history

The events of our own twentieth century give ample illustration of the fact that revival is frequently a prelude to judgement, and constitutes an expression of mercy prior to wrath. Perhaps one of the most outstanding examples of this in the Western world took place in the first two decades of the century. The first decade was one of extraordinary revival in many parts of the world. Edwin Orr estimated that something like five million people were converted to Christ worldwide. An amazing ingathering! As far as Britain was concerned, the revival had its greatest impact in Wales in 1904, and then spread out to other parts of the British Isles. Altogether about a million converts were brought into the churches. The next decade, however, saw the three great imperialist nations, Britain, France and Germany, along with others, engaged in a conflict which utterly destroyed the flower of their manhood in the most appalling carnage ever seen up to that point in history. Literally millions were killed. No family was left unbereaved. The accounts of the battlefield scenes are harrowing in the extreme. The legacy of injuries was enormous.

Historians, with their careful analyses of the political and economic causes of World War I, do not seek to uncover spiritual causes. The sword as the cup of God's wrath is for most of them never an acceptable concept. While many Christians would not deny the truth of such a concept, a great number of them would be more likely to see the World War I conflict in terms of moments of heroism or intense grief rather than in terms of judgement. The backcloth to Acts, as well as the testimony of Scripture generally, should, however, make us think more carefully here, and recognise with humility the real cause of that War.

In looking at the causes of the revival of 1900–1910 Edwin Orr asked the question, "Why did it occur at that time?" He suggested that "The prescient wisdom of its author may . . . account for the sudden spread of the Revival . . . Within ten years the awful slaughter of World War I had begun . . . The Awakening was a kind of harvest before the devastation of Christendom." In other words, God knew the carnage that had to come, and saved many for eternity before it happened. Orr went on to quote a more general statement from a biographer of the great evangelist, Wilbur Chapman: "In the history of revivals, it has often been noted that such restoral periods are a warning of, and synchronise with, impending judgement."

It is certainly the case that some of the areas of the world which have seen the most bloodshed, cruelty and oppression have also been areas in which God has moved with great revival power. The immense outpourings of the Spirit of God on Korea have come in a number of waves since the turn of the century, but there can be few countries that have gone through so many successive, destructive and vicious occupations as has that country. China also has suffered immensely through civil wars, Japanese occupation and ruthless dictatorships. Millions have died and suffering has been widespread. Yet that land has also been a land of revivals and spiritual harvests, and literally millions have found Christ. Korea boasts the largest church in the world, and China the largest ingathering of converts ever seen. When Wilbur Chapman's biographer wrote his reflections on the events at the turn of the century he said, "We cannot escape the conviction that God in gracious providence was reaping a spiritual harvest before He permitted the outburst of revolutionary forces that have overwhelmed the world." Those revolutionary forces have certainly caused untold bloodshed as the century has proceeded, but the harvests have just as certainly been reaped.

Another illustration of this connection between judgement and revival that springs to mind is that of the 1850s and 1860s in North America. Those years saw one of the most amazing movements of the Spirit of God ever to visit that continent, and yet at the same time they saw the appallingly bitter and extensive bloodshed of the American Civil War. They are perhaps best epitomised by the young D. L. Moody. In the late fifties he was part of a movement of the Spirit which brought hundreds of thousands of men into the Kingdom, but in the sixties he was among those who worked desperately to bring spiritual and social comfort to the vast numbers of young men who found themselves killing each other or suffering desperately in prison camps.

As long as we are in the world we shall be facing the fact that God's judgement must flow over peoples and countries where there has been flagrant sin. This is particularly so where gross inhumanity has been perpetrated by one group of people upon another. When men abuse each other with cruelty and hatred, there is an inevitable reaping of judgement. But equally true is the fact that as long as the Spirit of God is in the world there will be movements of grace and salvation mingling with those judgements. This fact is the all-important spur of hope which encourages us to seek the face of God, to believe for His mercy and to expect times of revival.

In our own times we certainly need to cling to this fact. The essential inhumanity of abortion as it is normally and openly practised, the promotion of the so-called "right" to be lesbian, homosexual or worse (and the consequent degradation of the very idea of rights), the widespread acceptance of occultism and the increase of violence and dishonesty are but a few of the features of our world which cry out for judgement. Our society is rapidly becoming nothing more than a re-run of Sodom; it increasingly resembles Paul's vivid description in Romans 2 of the pagan world, which was given over to its own lusts. It is already tasting the bitter fruits of its rebellion against God, but is none the less still wilfully rebelling. Judgement has already been pronounced: it is simply a question of what punishment God in His righteousness hands out, whether by sword or disease.

Yet nothing in this should ever cause us to cease to cry out to God for His visitations of mercy in revival power, and nothing should persuade us that God cannot and would not visit a country in such need. There is an abundance of evidence to give us hope here. It is not a cheap hope, and the evidence does not allow presumption for one moment. It is a hope that makes costly demands, but none the less it is hope, and it is real.

In considering this point Arthur Skevington Wood draws attention to the Protestant Reformation itself — one of the greatest periods of revival. He writes:

> Few could have guessed on the eve of the Protestant Reformation, that the gates of new life were to swing open so soon. The institutional church had apparently reached the nadir of corruption. The Pope was more a symbol of temporal power than of spiritual leadership. The curia was notorious for its immorality and love of luxury . . . the parish clergy were largely blind leaders of the blind. The

53

blatant materialism which had gripped the whole hierarchical system was epitomised in the campaign to popularise indulgences. Yet it was in the midst of such unlikely circumstances that God was about to visit His people . . .

The early eighteenth century is very frequently and rightly quoted as an era of appalling degradation morally, and gross indifference spiritually. Open immorality was to be seen among the royal family and the greatest leaders of the nation. Yet this was the century which saw the emergence of Wesley and Whitefield and many other powerful instruments of revival. It is interesting that even in Scotland in those days the Kirk had lost all its spiritual vitality, Arianism had reared its head and the prevailing theology provided only a system of morality. Despite a crying need for restoration, revival broke in.

Tom Shaw, writing a recent Foreword to John Weir's eyewitness account of the great 1859 revival in Ulster, expressed his view that the book "is one of those glorious accounts of how God visited Ulster with spiritual revival in a time of great religious declension and abounding immorality during the last century, producing a remarkable change in every area of life". He went on to say that but for such records, we might as well despair of our own situation at the end of the twentieth century. As long as such records are there, however, we have something on which to place our hope.

So to the Christian who has his heart open to God, a dark backcloth is never the signal for despair. We should never be amongst those who suppose that everything must get much worse as time gets closer to the Lord's return, and that an increase of God's wrath will eliminate blessing. As long as the Spirit is in the world, and God's people are stirred to seek His fullness, there will always be blessing. Despite all the judgements that threaten, the harvest fields have fuller crops than ever before, and it is time for reaping. Scripture and history point conclusively to this. If we are prepared to be stirred not merely with the great danger of the times in which we live, but also with the abounding mercy and the amazing power of God, then there is hope. The need is for the People of God to seek afresh this mercy and power.

We see that God is faithful and will never forget the promises He has made to His Church . . . even when the floods seem to be overwhelming it, but will revive it again, even in the darkest times.

Jonathan Edwards writing to George Whitefield

Chapter 4: Living Promise

You will be baptised in the Holy Spirit.

Acts 1:5

In the last days, God says, I will pour out my Spirit.

Joel 2:28

Some five weeks after Jesus had stood on the Mount of Olives and pronounced a word of judgement over Jerusalem, He stood on the same ground and pronounced a word of blessing. A glorious light was about to be superimposed on the dark backcloth. It came in the form of a promise. The promise was that His disciples were to receive the Holy Spirit, and that when the Spirit had come they would find themselves endued with power for effective witness, first in Jerusalem and then to the world outside. They were to become the instruments of widespread blessing to all sorts of people.

It is this word of promise that constitutes the real starting point of the apostolic outpouring. Everything that happened in Acts was the result of that promise. It is the first feature in the first chapter of Acts and must be the first thing we look at. It is the vital key to the divine blueprint. There would not have been, and there could not have been an outpouring of Holy Spirit blessing if God had not purposed it and announced it with a promise. In the same way there can be no hope of any subsequent outpourings without a similar promise.

The first chapter of Acts also makes it quite clear to us that the promise always precedes prayer. Prayer is not the first step to blessing. Jesus had to make the promise, and only then could the disciples "give themselves to prayer".

This is clearly the only possible sequence, for without the word of promise there is no basis for effective prayer. Prayer is an utterly crucial step in the accomplishment of the purposes of God, but it can never be more than an instrument for securing God's revealed purposes and can never go beyond His promises. If we pray outside His promises we pray in vain.

Thus if revival is not something to be found in the purposes and promises of God, we will be wasting our time when we pray for it — even if we pray incessantly. But if the promise which underlies our praying for revival is in fact the same promise which underlay the early apostolic outpouring, then our praying is well based and we can press forward with assured hope.

We need to ask two questions in particular, therefore, about this apostolic promise. First of all, was the promise which Jesus made something only for His immediate followers or was it also meant for our generation? Secondly, how much was encompassed in the promise? How wide were the implications of it? Did it imply all that we think of when we consider revival?

A promise for us

The answer to the first question is, of course, crucial. Are we right in assuming that the promise that Jesus made about the Spirit extends beyond the apostolic age? Are we correct in looking for the same sort of fulfilment in our own time? Was there a special dimension of its fulfilment meant only for the early Church? If the answer is a negative, then we need go no further. But quite clearly it must be a very positive affirmative.

If we have any doubts as to whether we stand today in the same relation to that promise as the disciples did, we need only to listen to Peter's preaching on the Day of Pentecost. He reminded his audience of the words of Joel: " 'In the last days,' says God, 'I will pour out my Spirit' " (Acts 2:17). The expression "in the last days" certainly does not refer only to the apostolic times. It refers to the whole dispensation of the Spirit of which the apostolic era was but a beginning. Peter clearly understood it in this way, for he concluded his preaching by reminding his hearers that the promise was "for them and for their children and for as many as call on the name of the Lord" (2:39). Today we are in the "last days". The promise is still with us, meant for us and relevant to us. It was meant to ring not merely through the Book of Acts but through the whole history of the Church. If we deny that, we deny the most fundamental of truths.

Furthermore, we can only conclude that when the promise was made, its full potential must have been included in it. We are not made a half promise or a part promise, but we are offered the whole promise. All the possibilities and ramifications of the promise as we see them in Acts are now offered to us. One wonders just how much of the full potential and experience of that promise has been lost because of sincere but none the less misguided theological misgivings about how much is available.

If, then, anyone should ask the question, "What right have we to pray for revival?" or "What exactly is it we are praying for when we pray for revival?" the answer is that we are praying on the basis of a promise that has been beckoning us on from apostolic times, and we are praying for nothing less than a fulfilment of it of apostolic proportions.

A promise with great implications

We may turn, therefore, to our second question and ask what those apostolic proportions were. What precisely did the promise encompass? It is very important to understand this because, even if we were assured that it was a promise for us now in our time, we could so underestimate the implications of it that we could in fact receive only part of what was intended. We could become satisfied with something very much less than the whole.

61

This warning holds true even if the account in Acts leaves us feeling that the disciples themselves could not have fully understood all the implications of what was being promised by Jesus. I doubt, for instance, whether they would have been looking for supernatural manifestations of wind and fire, or of tongues. I doubt whether they would have envisaged the extraordinary boldness that was to fall on them for the task of witnessing. All of which means that it is possible to lay hold of a promise and to receive something which is way beyond one's understanding. Many have doubtless experienced precisely this when they have prayed for the Spirit. But it remains true, none the less, that in many instances failure to comprehend the full implications of the promise has meant that people have actually been unable to hold on to some of what has been given them, losing the blessing through sheer ignorance. In other instances ignorance of the full measure and nature of what God intended has led to an outright rejection of spiritual blessing even as it has begun to be manifested. Finally we have to take note of the fact that in the Kingdom we normally receive what we ask for, and we need to have in mind all that is being offered by God as we pray. Certainly, in our position, on this side of Pentecost, we need to take advantage of what we can know, and there can be no doubt that proper knowledge does make the pathway to the fulfilment of God's promise much more sure.

The promise itself, as it comes to us from the lips of Jesus, is really very brief. He simply said, "You will be baptised in the Holy Spirit" and "You will receive power when the Holy Spirit comes upon you and you will be my witnesses . . ." (Acts 1:5,8). The brevity of these words should not, however, blind us to the enormous implications and impact that they were to have.

The very words themselves are pregnant with implications. Take for instance the expression, "baptised in the Spirit". Whatever one's own personal viewpoint may be about what baptism in the Spirit is, one thing must be beyond dispute, and that is that the word "baptism" was referring to something that was a very significant and comprehensive experience. When someone is baptised in water they are either plunged beneath its surface or they are drenched completely by having it poured all over them. The word "baptise" is not a word of half measure. To receive a "baptism in the Spirit" means to experience a complete and total immersion in the Spirit. There is a sense of completeness, fullness and totality about it.

The implications of the promise are best understood, however, not so much by the terminology used but by what actually happened as the promise was fulfilled. The disciples were indeed drenched with the Spirit. When they received the "baptism" they recognised immediately that there was now a great River flowing within their lives. They really were "full" of the Spirit. Boldness, love, praise and joy all flowed out of them, and they knew the "enabling" had come. God chose to signify all this by "the blowing of a violent wind from heaven" and by tongues of fire that "separated and came to rest on each of them". These last two features may well have been outward symbols of more important inner realities, but they are symbols which speak of something very powerful and unmistakable. Likewise, at a later stage, as some were praying together, "the place where they were meeting was shaken". Something quite remarkable was happening. They were full, they were on fire, God was moving in power and they knew it. They were drenched! They were deeply conscious of the Spirit, not as a doctrinal formulation to which they gave assent, but as a very real Presence and Power within them.

They found also that this great flood of the Holy Spirit was flowing not merely within them but also around them. As they moved in His power *to* the world, He moved with equal power *on* the world to make their witness of great consequence. The promise was working itself out in great preaching, conviction, miracles and witness. It was a very big promise, wide in scope and powerful in its consequences.

We can get a still better grasp of the nature and extent of the promise when we compare the spiritual state of the disciples before the Pentecostal outpouring with their state after it. Prior to Pentecost the disciples had already had a deep spiritual experience. They exhibited a clear faith in Jesus. They had seen Him rise from the dead and were committed to following and obeying Him, despite what had happened at the Crucifixion. They had been thoroughly taught about the purpose of the Crucifixion and had at last come to understand that it was an essential part of the Messiah's mission. Jesus had actually breathed the Spirit over them to enable them to pronounce forgiveness in His name. They were bonded together to a high degree. They had certainly "seen" the Kingdom of God and had been taught through the Spirit. But now, after Pentecost, there was a completely new dimension: a dimension of spiritual "power". They knew the Holy Spirit was flowing in fullness and that He was making them a force to be reckoned with. They really knew the meaning of the words "power", "baptism" and "anointing". They were moving with a divine tide; they were not struggling, with just their own resources at their disposal. They had been impacted and the world was being impacted through them. There was a great consciousness among them of the presence of the Spirit.

These then, were the ramifications of the promise. It is the essential purpose of this book to explore them in detail. At this point it is imperative to grasp that we are talking about a promise with huge implications and far-reaching consequences. Its fulfilment was not in any sense mild or barely noticeable. It was completely transforming. It would be quite wrong to dilute the import of the promise and to think that it simply means, for example, a coming of the Spirit to indwell. The emphasis is clearly on an outflowing not just an indwelling. The promise did very much more than change the disciples' lives in a marginal way. It was a promise which in its very essence spoke of "baptism" or "fullness" or "empowering". It was a promise not of partial power but of the fullness of power. Moreover, it was not a promise which was confined only to the spiritual welfare of the disciples; rather, it constituted a great surge of divine activity whereby thousands were brought into the Kingdom of God. It was a promise which, as it was fulfilled, brought into being the mighty awakening in Jerusalem and lit the flame which touched whole areas of the Mediterranean world within a few short years.

It is this same apostolic promise, with all the vast potential that it implies, which has been at the heart of all succeeding outpourings of the Spirit. Revival always begins with a grasp of the true nature and wide extent of this promise. We need to read this promise not at its lowest level of fulfilment, or even at the level of our own experience; instead we must read it at the level of its biblical fulfilment. We must not pull down the promise to the limits of our own horizons; rather, we should allow those horizons to be extended to all the possibilities that God holds out to us. Only then do we enter into the full measure of the promise.

A longstanding promise

It would be perfectly true to say, therefore, that when it comes to seeking God for revival we do not need any promise other than that which Jesus made. The true fulfilment of that promise is revival, for revival is the coming of the Spirit in the full flow of His power.

In making this statement, however, we do need to recognise the fact that Jesus Himself was conscious of bringing to the forefront a promise that already had a long pedigree. He was not announcing something that had never been heard before. It had, in fact, been on the pages of prophecy for many centuries, and He had spoken previously to His disciples about "the Promise" to which the Old Testament bore witness. Indeed, it was at the Feast of Tabernacles, with its great symbolism of the outpouring of the Spirit, that He had cried out publicly that he would be the one who would fulfil the Promise (John 7:37–39). His unique contribution was to be precisely that. He, and He alone, was now to make the promise of the Spirit a reality.

But it was a promise that had been long embedded in the Old Testament record.

This means that the New Testament revival promise has an enormous wealth of Old Testament parallels. When we look at our blueprint, we should not be surprised, therefore, to find that no sooner had the promised Spirit been outpoured than Peter was explaining it and describing it in terms of a fulfilment of an Old Testament prophecy. To Peter it was "that which was spoken by the prophet Joel" (Acts 2:16) — it was the pouring out of the Spirit in the last days. The new experience of the Spirit was throwing a flood of light on the old prophetic word, and the old prophetic word was throwing a flood of light on the new experience.

This explanation of the Pentecostal outpouring in terms of Old Testament prophecy is certainly a characteristic which has been constantly repeated amongst all those who have been caught up in revival or in the longing for it. The coming of the Spirit in great power had been indeed the "desert blossoming as the rose" (Isaiah 35:1), "the floods coming on the dry ground" (44:3), "God marching before His people" (Psalm 68:7), the scattering of His enemies (68:1), "the seeing of the glory of the Lord, the majesty of our God (45:4), and so on. Nothing less that the imagery of the prophets seems to give adequate expression to the nature of the full outpouring of the Spirit.

It is a general principle of Scripture that Old Testament pictures teach us a great deal about the implications of New Testament statements. Thus when we look carefully at those pictures we are left in no doubt that revival is a time when God comes in His glory and majesty and reveals Himself. It is a time when He pours fresh spiritual life into dry and dead churches. It is a time when He cuts through the wilderness with a pathway of holiness and insists that His people walk along it (Isaiah 35:8ff). It is a time when the redeemed return to Him with singing and everlasting joy (35:10). It is a time when godly men grow up like great trees and once again cover the land (41:19). It is, moreover, a time in which God puts to flight the kings and principalities

66

which seek to stand in the way of His purposes (Psalm 68:14). It is a time of great proclamation of the Word of truth (68:11). And it is a time which is the consequence of a great thirst and longing amongst God's people for His favour (Isaiah 41:17ff).

There is in fact not one single aspect of revival blessing which is omitted in these great pictures. They are of immense value to us as we try to gain on understanding of revival, and they can only bring a new depth to our appreciation of it. They need to be the subject of much meditation.

Again it should not surprise us, therefore, that frequently people are made alive to the revival promise not through the words of Jesus but through some Old Testament prophetic word concerning the Spirit. Moreover, when it comes to earnest prayer for revival, the language and expression which inevitably comes again and again to the heart and lips is that of the prophetic imagery.

Responding to the promise

Whether we grasp the revival promise through the words of Jesus or through the Old Testament prophetic word, the whole crux of the matter as far as the people of God are concerned is how clearly that promise is perceived, how deeply its implications are appreciated and how earnestly it is sought after. This promise is no different from any other promise of God. To become effective, it has to become meaningful. It has to be taken to heart and pursued with confident faith. If we do not perceive the promise of God with any clarity and we are blinded to it for one reason or another, we are not going to pursue it. If we do not pursue it, we are not going to enter into it. Likewise, if our understanding of its fulfilment is incomplete and we become mistakenly satisfied with a partial fulfilment, we are not going to pursue it to the extent we should, and the result is that we are not going to see the fullest blessing. In other words, this promise, like all the promises of God, needs to be "quickened" or "made alive" to our hearts. Or, if you prefer, it needs to be "rediscovered". Only then does it become of consequence.

When Jesus first uttered the promise to His disciples, it obviously came over to them in precisely this kind of meaningful way. It became very much alive to their hearts. Jesus was speaking directly and personally to them. He meant every word He said, and they knew it. It came over to them also as something that was speaking to their inner need. For undoubtedly they must have been deeply conscious of the enormity of the task He was giving them, expecting them to "make disciples of all nations", and they must have felt anything but able to put it into effect. An "enabling" was something that they very much wanted to hear about, and it was just such an enabling that the promise was offering. It came over, therefore, in a manner which was both demanding and appealing. It immediately turned their hearts to expectant prayer.

A promise is of no consequence whatsoever if it is not alive and creating this kind of vibrant expectancy. The tragedy of so much of our Christian life is that the promise and purposes of God very frequently do not come over to us with anything like that degree of clarity and relevance with which they came to those who first received them. What we need is not just a promise, but a living promise.

The ability to receive that kind of clarity calls, of course, for a great deal of prayerful waiting upon God and meditation in the word — a brand of spirituality which the pressures of the modern world rapidly push out of our lives. Revelation of the purposes of God is the greatest need of true spirituality, and time and quietness are essential for that revelation.

We should also take careful note of the fact that we are involved in a very real fight with powers of darkness whose great aim it is to thwart the purposes and blessings of God in every possible way. If the starting-point of blessing is to be found in the promises of God, every effort is going to be made by the enemy to bury these promises, or to blight them or minimise them. As long as men are kept ignorant of the promises' true import, they cannot take root and bear their fruit. In this battle the forces of darkness find a very willing ally in our flesh, with all its inherent complacency and its ready tendency to run along the comfortable ruts of old traditions.

Certainly, no promise is more bitterly opposed than that which has to do with the coming of the Holy Spirit in the fullness of His power. Such a coming means the destruction of the Kingdom of Darkness. It means life for men, death for Satan. There is, therefore, a constant effort to take away this promise, and if it cannot be taken away, to throw on it as much confusion and misrepresentation as possible. It is no accident that some of the greatest battles in the Church have been fought over the promise of the Spirit! In this, one of the most persistent tactics of the enemy has been to pit Christian against Christian, injecting hardness, misunderstanding and dogmatism wherever possible. This is something we must never cease to be aware of and seek at all costs to avoid.

Not surprisingly, therefore, when we come to look at the history of revivals we find that it is always, amongst other things, a history of the quickening or rediscovery of the original Pentecostal promise and vision. Revivals have always come into being when the people of God have grasped afresh that God's purpose is a Spirit-filled Church moving with power, and have then sought to lay hold of the promise of the Spirit.

It has not always been the case, however, that the revival vision has been perceived or rediscovered through direct reading of the promise of the Spirit in Scripture. Again and again Christians have been unable to grasp the full import of the Bible's message, and God has had to draw their attention to some lifesize situation in which the promise was actually made a reality. Then, and only then, do they begin to realise the immense importance and scope of the promise. What we find, therefore, is that in the vast majority of cases people come to a rediscovery of the truth about the Spirit and revival through hearing or reading a testimony of how

His power has been released in revival somewhere in the world. The impact of such testimony is frequently very powerful indeed, and it is this which causes an immediate reappraisal of the biblical promises. Let me repeat this statement: the vast majority of people come to acquire the vision of revival through reading or hearing an account of revival. This has always been the most important means of promoting it.

For example, as far back as the early eighteenth century Jonathan Edwards felt he should write some short accounts of God's outpouring of the Spirit in his own area of New England.[1] When these accounts crossed the Atlantic they caused a longing among some in Britain that the same kind of outpouring should be witnessed here, and they caused a new expectation that it would indeed happen. Those who were so aroused gave themselves to prayer, and were not disappointed. This was particularly the case in Scotland, where a series of revivals ensued. Likewise, reports of the Welsh Revival of 1904 sent ripples of fresh vision and expectation to many parts of India and the Far East. As individuals in those areas caught sight of the promise of God through the testimony of His work in Wales, so the outpourings spread in their own more remote parts of the world.

There is yet a further way in which God seeks to bring home the relevance and importance of His purposes and promises, and that is through the prophetic gift. This prophetic gift is intended to bring to the people of God a forceful reminder of those divine decrees and promises which are particularly relevant to them but which they are either only dimly perceiving or blatantly ignoring. The gift functions when God is seeking to rouse His people to fall into line more closely with His purposes. The true prophetic Word always strongly underlines the relevance and immediacy of some aspect of the revealed or written Word and awakens the Church to it. It may come through powerful exposition and the application of biblical passages, or it may come through a more "charismatic" and direct pronouncement.

We are certainly living in an age when God has added this

prophetic element to contemporary testimony in order to stir and to encourage His people to lay hold of the promise of the outpouring of the Spirit. The last few decades in Britain have heard both powerful preaching and numerous and independent prophetic utterances of the "charismatic" type which have pointed unmistakably to the fact that it is very much still in the purpose of God to fulfil the apostolic promise in all its aspects, and not least in Britain.[2]

Perhaps the most remarkable of these utterances was made by Smith Wigglesworth, the Pentecostal evangelist. I quote what is probably one of the most authentic reconstructions of that prophetic word:

> There is a revival coming that at present the world knows nothing about. It will come through the churches. It will come in a fresh way. When you see what God does in this revival you will then have to admit that all you have seen previously is a mere nothing in comparison with what is to come. It will eclipse anything that has been known in history. Empty churches, empty cathedrals, will be packed again with worshippers. Buildings will not be able to accommodate the multitudes. Then you will see fields of people worshipping and praising together.[3]

Such prophetic activity needs thoroughly weighing, of course, and at the end of the day it does not provide us with the true basis of our hope − only the promise in the Scriptures can do that. None the less, its contributory stimulus to what is a biblically based promise is something that we should be very foolish to ignore. We are called not only to test the prophets, but also to believe them so that we may be established.

Notes

1. Jonathan Edwards, *A Narrative of Surprising Conversions. The distinguishing Marks of a Work of the Spirit of God. An Account of the Revival of Religion in Northampton 1740−42.*

2. For example:

H. Brash Bonsall received a direct word of God in 1931 to the effect that He would send a great revival to Britain, and that Brash Bonsall's part in it would be Bible college work. This led to life-long work with students and to the creation of the Birmingham Bible Institute.

In 1953 Derek Prince received a word from God (experiencing it as an "audible voice") that a great revival was to come both in America and in Britain. This word was so real that it caused him to pray consistently for revival from that time onward, and it was still strongly with him in 1989.

When he was a Bible college student Bryn Jones received an extraordinary revelation in which he saw a great ingathering of people into the Kingdom of God. It came to him in the form of a trance and was confirmed by his subsequent experiences.

Jean Darnell received a vision from God of an increasing number of lights in Britain, all of which would gather together before a lightning bolt of revival would move through the country, passing over into Europe. This vision produced a life-long ministry in Britain.

Charles Slagle received a vision in which he saw God moving over Britain with lava fire. From Britain it moved onto the continent, and then burst out into other parts of the world. This vision was repeated in the early hours of the morning each day for a week. God had since expanded Slagle's ministry in Britain.

There are numerous others on record. The ones I have quoted are particularly strong for three reasons: first, they are unrelated to each other; secondly, they have each been vindicated by prolific ministries that have sprung out of them; and thirdly they have not merely persisted but have grown in the convictions of those concerned.

3. Peter Hocken, *Streams of Renewal*, p. 19.

Faith is the key that unlocks the door of God's power. "By faith the walls of Jericho fell down." And in revival work one of the indispensable prerequisites is a living, vital Faith. "All things are possible to him that believeth."

The man who is to be used of the Lord will hear from Heaven. God will give him a promise. . . . Some familiar promise, it may be, will suddenly grip him in such a way that he will know God has spoken. Hence if I would attempt a new work for God, let me ask myself first of all the questions: "Have I a promise? Has God spoken?"

Oswald J. Smith

Chapter 5: Crucial Response (1)

All these with one accord devoted themselves to prayer.

Acts 1:14

After the risen Jesus had made His promise to send the Spirit and had ascended to His Father, the disciples went back to Jerusalem and gave themselves to prayer. This lasted for ten days. They were still in the place of prayer when on the day of Pentecost the promise was fulfilled and the Spirit was poured out. Those ten days, so carefully noted in the first chapter of Acts, amply indicate one of the most clearly grasped truths about the nature of revival, namely that it invariably comes out of earnest prayer.

This truth holds out one simple challenge: if we are serious about revival, then we have to make up our minds to give ourselves to pray for it. There is no alternative. It happens no other way. Writing about the 1860 revival in Ireland, Tom Shaw said: "It began when God moved upon the hearts of a small group of people, resulting in a prayer burden that never slackened until God rent the Heavens, and mountains of sin and evil flowed down at His presence".[1] The same could be said about any revival.

In the first chapter of Acts there is a clear promise-prayer-fulfilment sequence which is divinely ordained and which is never broken. In Acts 1:8 Jesus makes the promise, in 1:14 the disciples respond in prayer and in 2:1 the fulfilment comes. This means we can never take the view that a promise made by God will be fulfilled automatically. In order to be fulfilled the promise will need to lodge deep in some heart somewhere and become the burden of earnest prayer. Whenever an outpouring of the Spirit is witnessed, prayer

75

will have preceded it. It is the great essential link between promise and fulfilment. Promises remain only promises until we respond to them in prayer.

There are three vital features about this prayer which our apostolic blueprint makes plain. All of them have been present whenever an adequate prayer response has been made to the challenge of revival. First, the disciples' prayer was believing prayer; then it was united prayer; finally it was persistent prayer. That is the threefold challenge which we need to look at in this chapter and in the succeeding ones.

The priority of faith

It is right to begin with believing prayer — prayer which expresses real faith. When God makes a promise He looks for one thing above everything else, and that is a response of faith. He simply wants to hear an unclouded "I believe what You say!" Abraham became the father of many nations because he believed God's promise (Genesis 15:5–7). On the other hand, a whole generation of Israelites missed the Promised Land because they would not believe what God said (Hebrews 3:19). There is no greater response than faith, and there is no greater failure than unbelief — "Without faith it is impossible to please God" (11:6). Even obedience follows on from faith. Works are crucial, but to be acceptable they must spring out of faith. Faith is the great starting-point of all blessing, the essential requirement of the Gospel itself.

When faith is exercised in response to a promise, then no matter what may be the difficulties or seeming impossibilities that stand in the way, a fulfilment of the promise is sure. It may well require patience and much heart-searching in addition, but the starting-point is found in that moment when faith is born. Such faith is basic to the prayer that prevails for revival. Above all else we must believe the promise, and believe it with that degree of clarity that enables the utmost perseverance. It is when people thoroughly grasp the fact that outpourings of the Spirit

76

really are in God's mind and then begin to express faith for their occurrence that the prospects for revival become bright. This is the paramount precondition of revival — a firm, believing grip on the full promise of the Spirit expressed in heartfelt prayer.

It is for this reason, of course, that we must focus on the promise of the Spirit, drink it deep into our hearts and dispel any doubts which would cloud its truth and reality. If we are not affirming the promise of revival in fullness of faith we are not likely to see it materialise.

The kind of faith we are talking about here is really something which God Himself breathes into our hearts. We are speaking of a process in which the meaning and relevance of a promise of God is made so clear and obvious to us by the Spirit that we know at a deep level that it is true and that God wants it to be fulfilled. Some of us undoubtedly will have experienced times in our lives when a promise made by God in His Word has taken on a particular freshness and meaning. These will have been times when something with which we are fairly familiar becomes personal, urgent and demanding. Such moments frequently take us by surprise, and can even cause a sense of fearfulness, but we recognise immediately a divine imprint. We wonder why we have never seen it quite so clearly before. Our hearts are drawn to the promise and, despite our apprehensions, become enlarged in faith for its fulfilment. Something of an inner compulsion is born to grasp at what is being offered, even if we cannot fully understand it. These are moments of enormous consequence, for they are the moments of true response, of the birth of that responsive faith that can bring about a fulfilment of what is being promised. This kind of faith may be rightly called "God-breathed faith".

It is precisely this quickening activity of the Holy Spirit that has been at the root of true revival prayer right from the very start. This warming of faith in the promise of the outpouring of the Spirit has in fact come with such frequency and in so many different places in the world that it affords one of the clearest indicators of God's lasting desire to give the Spirit in power. Such faith has been the constant forerunner of revival.

Take one simple example. Jonathan Goforth was an outstanding missionary in China when, at the age of forty-five he received news of the Welsh revival of 1904. This coincided with a period in which a "strange restlessness seemed to take possession of him" and in which his heart yearned for "greater works". Having read eagerly of what was happening in Wales, his response was to search through as much other material on revival as he could find. Even more important, he began to spend hours with his Bible, absorbed in an intensive study of the Holy Spirit. This he did on his knees. His wife disturbed him one morning, anxious over the intensity of his search. He replied, "I feel like one who has tapped a mine of wealth! It is so wonderful! If only I could get others to see it!" The "it" he was referring to was the promise and truth of revival, now intensely alive to him through his studies. Having grasped hold of the vision, he held to it with much faith and prayer. He eagerly shared it with his Chinese workers, who in their turn felt the same quickening of faith. The outcome was that by 1908 he was witnessing some astonishing outpourings of the Spirit as he preached throughout Manchuria.[2]

This quickening of the promise of the Spirit is not only fundamental to initiating prevailing prayer for revival, but also gives us the vital clue when we come to consider the question of the right time to pray for revival. Some are held back from praying because they sincerely want to know what is the right time in the sovereign will of God to pray for it. They do not feel happy to pray until they are sure on that score. In response to that we must insist that when praying for revival springs out of enlivened faith and is a response to deep inner Holy Spirit promptings, then we know we are moving with God's timetable. Such prayer is never out of tune or out of time with God's plans, and transcends academic discussions concerning God's sovereignty. Such prayer is, in fact, prompted by God's sovereign purposes. We need to recognise that a sure barometer of God's timing concerning any of His purposes is the level of vision and heart-concern which He has imparted to His people for that particular purpose. Revelation, vision, heart-concern and desire are due primarily and essentially to the stirrings of the Holy Spirit. These are the means by which He moves His people to accomplish His purposes. He makes sure that such promptings find lodging in receptive hearts when He is about to bring those purposes into being.

We need to remember also, in this connection, that we cannot say people are wrong in their praying for revival simply because they have been praying for a long time without apparent results. The "right time" to pray for revival is not always necessarily to be judged by the swiftness of the answer to prayer. Marie Monsen, a missionary powerfully used by God in China in the early years of this century, prayed for revival for nearly twenty years before it came.[3] Should she have started ten years later? Would she have been wrong to have prayed even if she had never seen revival? Obviously not! As we shall see in a later chapter, many prayed for the world-wide spread of the Gospel long before anything like a fulfilment was noticed, but they were certainly not out of line with the will of God. The prompting that produces believing prayer may well come many years before fulfilment. If, then, we are tempted to say that prayer for revival is not always answered, we need to ask ourselves immediately how long we are going to give God to answer our prayer. We would do well to think of Abraham waiting for the birth of Isaac.

The birthpangs of faith

Whilst we affirm that enlivened faith, the God-prompted response to the promise of the Spirit, is of the greatest importance in bringing about the outpourings of the Spirit, we should, however, take very good note of the fact that the pathway to such clear faith is not always easy. The promises of God rarely become meaningful unless one's heart has been painfully stretched in some way or another

79

beforehand. The promise of the Spirit has been grasped most fully by those who have felt most acutely the need for deeper personal blessing and for a greater God-given power in their work. It has been in the long periods of wrestling over those needs that revelation has come. The Spirit is actually promised to those who are thirsty. It is "when the poor and needy seek for water" that "rivers are opened on the dry ground" (Isaiah 44:3; 35:6—7). This means that very frequently the road to an appreciation of the promise is a pathway of travail and even pain. It is a pathway of deepening discontent, sometimes of heartbreak. It is out of a personal wilderness or out of a sense of the barrenness of the work in which one is engaged that the heart begins to struggle towards a realisation of what God has promised by the Spirit. It is when complacency is broken and we can no longer bear the dryness of the present situation that God can, through His Word, begin to direct our attention to the remedy, and to show us that it lies in the person of the Holy Spirit.

Marie Monsen, mentioned above, is very much a case in point here. As a young missionary she found herself struggling with a major problem. Her heart told her that God could do tremendous things through faith. The biographies of George Muller and Hudson Taylor had convinced her of that. In addition, the great happenings in the Book of Acts were a constant stimulus in the same direction. On the other hand, however, her fellow missionaries were insisting that China was different from anywhere else, and that no great, powerful work could be expected there except over a long period of time. She wrestled for several years with the deep frustrations of this conflict, wondering how much she really could expect God to do. In the midst of this turmoil she heard about the revival in Korea and the great ingathering of converts there (1907). She wanted to go to see what was happening. She hoped in some way to touch the secret of that revival and bring it to China. However, God then gave this word to her: "What you want through that journey you may be given here, where you are, in answer to prayer." Faith began to rise immediately and she began to pray for a similar outpouring of the Spirit where she was. At that point she found herself the object of a direct satanic assault. This, however, only served to confirm her belief in the rightness of her requests. She now knew beyond any doubt that the Spirit was promised to all and that He was, and would be, the answer to her deepest heart-longings for China.[4] Years of pain had produced prevailing faith. Great revivals followed.

Prayer for revival may well have its origins, therefore, in the depths of a divine discontent which disturbs our hearts. Such discontent will be characterised by earnest cries for help, by protestations that we cannot go on any longer, by longings that are indeed too deep for words, by bewilderment and even despair. There will be a constant lament over our human inadequacy and the shortcomings of self-effort. It is to those who are broken and humbled in this profound way that revelation of the promise will normally come.

We need to say also that within this travail, there may well be moments of particular pain when the Spirit of God strives to break us of self-seeking, pride and personal ambitions. We will be brought to an end of ourselves, to a point of brokenness and repentance over our attitudes and life-style, and to a moment when we are ready to allow God alone to dictate our way forward. These will be moments not of easy, formalised repentance, but of true heart breaking which will produce radical changes in our attitudes and behaviour. This is another constant forerunner of the outpouring of the Spirit.

I do not think it too fanciful to see something of this painful process happening amongst the apostles in the weeks before Pentecost. The Cross was a devastating blow to them, especially to Peter. The perplexity, bewilderment and sense of inadequacy which it brought to them must have persisted even after the Resurrection, and made them feel their need of a Comforter. That appalling exposure of their own weakness left them only too ready to grasp that glowing truth of the coming of the Spirit when it was finally confirmed to them by Jesus just before He ascended.

It is a general purpose of God to bring us through our inner struggles to that place where we may come face to face with His promises and respond in faith. When the struggle is about spiritual barrenness, the promise we meet is that of the Spirit. Once we understand the full scope of that promise, and faith for powerful outpourings of the Spirit is born, then in large measure the prayer which will begin to flow will be simply an expression of that faith. Struggle will give way to glad assertions concerning the faithfulness of God. We shall pray, believing, and with a well-founded hope. There will always be a note of praise, thanksgiving and expectancy in that prayer.

Undoubtedly this was a keynote of the praying in the upper room of which we read in Acts 1. Though we are not told in detail the nature of the prayer on that occasion, we can surely assume that the disciples spent a good deal of time in simply giving expression to their conviction that Jesus would do as He had promised and send the Spirit. After all, it was the promise of the Spirit that prompted the prayer, so there would have been many exclamations such as "We know You will do what You said", "We believe You are the Messiah", "We know You have ascended to Your Father in order to send the Spirit", and "We thank You for Your great purposes, and bless You that You will accomplish them". I would imagine that such exclamations would have been frequently punctuated by song and praise. That would have been a very natural way in which to express strong faith. From time to time, perhaps, there would have been moments in which they would have built up their faith further by reflecting carefully on precisely what Jesus had said about the Spirit — not simply what He had said just before His ascension, but also what He had said during the Last Supper and at other significant moments of His ministry. And the more they were edified by the vision of the Spirit, the more they would have expressed believing expectation of His coming.

Prayer for revival and the outpouring of the Spirit may have a number of stages and aspects, but central to it all must be this simple expression of faith in the promise. Doubt, fears, accusations and the like must not be allowed to cloud this essential thrust. God delights to hear declarations concerning His faithfulness. He loves to hear His people rejoice in the integrity of His Word. He loves to hear His truth proclaimed. He delights to hear faith claiming the Spirit in all His power.

It is precisely this determined attitude of faith in the promise of the Spirit coming in power that has been at the heart of the revivals which God has sent over the centuries.

I do not think it can be emphasised enough that revival does not spring out of a lukewarm interest in the subject. It can only spring out of a clear faith-grasp of God's desire to send it, a faith-grasp which in turn has sprung out of deep heart-longings for a powerful work of God. That sort of faith is our greatest need at the moment.

Obstacles to faith

There are, however, many obstacles to faith. It is a sad fact that frequently the barriers to faith are theological. When Jonathan Edwards sent out his famous call for united prayer for outpourings of the Spirit and for the world-wide spreading of the Gospel, he found himself driven to write far more than he had wanted to write, simply because he had to expose so many theological misrepresentations of prophecy that were undermining live faith in God's promises of the Spirit. People interpreted the prophetic scriptures as forecasting unparalleled doom and judgement, overlooking their emphasis on the mercy of God moving amongst those judgements and bringing widespread salvation and a harvesting of souls. This outlook was a stranglehold on faith and it had to be broken.[5]

If that was the battle of the eighteenth century, the battle of the nineteenth was, as we saw in Chapter 2, against those who loudly protested at any strong crying out for the Spirit, maintaining that He had already come among His people and that no more of His power was needed. That theological barrier was compounded by the refusal of many to countenance as biblical any desire for the Spirit to move with apostolic gifts. These were huge obstacles to the faith that brings revival.

In our own generation we also need to resist any similar theological attitudes that undermine and dispel heartfelt cries of faith for revival outpourings. Some of the attitudes just mentioned still remain in places. More to be guarded against, however, is an attitude which almost tends to make revival a matter more of our works than of God's grace. This tends to be the case when people present a seemingly never-ending list of pre-conditions for revival. Certainly, promises have conditions, but we need to be careful that we do not wrongly multiply those conditions. The essential conditions for revival are a broken heart and a humble faith. God can move very powerfully with those.[6]

In concluding this section on faith, it seems important to recognise the fact that expressing a promise which faith has grasped is not always an activity of unclouded praise. There is a fight of faith, and no matter how clearly an initial promise may come to the heart, there are times when there is a real struggle to hold to it. This is why constant affirmation and mutual encouragement is so vital. The Spirit had been promised to the disciples, but any unrealistic euphoria would have been immediately challenged by the fact that they were being called to witness in Jerusalem. The power of the authorities and their implacable hatred of Jesus would be facts fresh enough in the disciples' memories to raise all sorts of fears and questions. Awful moments of doubt can assail even the clearest grasp of God's promises. One would seriously doubt any testimony to the contrary. Yet, handled properly, those very moments, driving us back to further and even deeper wrestling with God, can ultimately give us an even firmer grip on the promise.

Prayer for witnessing

The expression of faith was not the only feature of the disciples' prayer in those days prior to Pentecost. There were other areas of prayer that grew out of their faith, and were prompted by the implications of the promise. Despite the lack of information on details, one thing is certain about those days — the disciples were seeking to prepare themselves for witness, and much prayer and thought was devoted to this. This is shown by the appointment of Matthias as an apostle during this period. Whether that appointment was right may be a matter of debate for some, but the fact that it happened shows a very real desire among the apostles to be in no way lacking numerically for the work of witness that lay ahead. Peter's concern over this is made very clear. As he looked at those who were eligible to take the place of Judas, he said, "One of these men must become with us a witness of his resurrection" (Acts 1:22). Witness was uppermost in his mind. He had obviously taken very seriously Jesus' remarks that the coming of the Spirit would herald a time of witness. He believed it, and out of his belief grew a desire to be ready.

Such preparation became the subject of much prayer. The inspiration to replace Judas and complete the apostolic band evidently came from the book of Psalms (Acts 1:20). It may well have been the case that Peter was directed to this as they waited on God. Direction of this kind is common during such times of prayer. When it came to deciding whom to choose, earnest prayer was made and the lot was cast in the presence of the Lord. The lot fell to Matthias, and so he was appointed.

All this points to the fact that a substantial part of the time they spent in prayer would have been taken up with getting prepared in heart and mind for all that the promise implied. "We need to seek God in order to be ready for the work we've got to do" would have been the prevailing attitude. This should prompt us when we are praying for revival to use a sanctified imagination to pray into all the things we are likely to find ourselves doing when God pours out His Spirit. For us, as for the disciples, sharing the experiences we have had and the testimonies we have heard of the activity of the Spirit in previous or contemporary revivals should become a crucial part of the whole prayer process. As we consider these experiences and testimonies in the place of prayer God is able to clarify our expectations, help us to anticipate problems, strengthen us to face difficulties and prepare us for the unexpected things that revival so often brings.

One wonders, for example, how the disciples might have sought to grapple in prayer with the clear commission to be witnesses in Samaria, which they had received from Jesus. Perhaps the apostles might have shared with the rest of the disciples the experiences they had had when Jesus had taken them to Samaria. On one occasion, at least, He had rebuked them for their hostile attitude to the Samaritans, making it quite clear that such an attitude showed that they did not understand the nature of the Spirit who was directing them. This might well have come to mind and led the disciples to humble themselves and repent afresh, and to cry out for the love of Jesus. It would certainly be the case that if they were to take the commission to the Samaritans seriously there would have to be much prayer about it.

Perhaps they found both that and the challenge of the ends of the earth a little too much to grasp at that point. They might well have found more than enough matter for prayer in their wrestling with the call to have the courage and boldness to witness to Jerusalem and its rulers. Whatever they focused on most, this was certainly a time for heart-searching and prayerful personal preparation.

It is good to pause as we contemplate this and ask ourselves this question: How earnestly do we pray for the power of the Spirit to enable the Church to witness as it did in those early days? Earnest prayer for revival will never be dissociated from earnest prayer for the spirit of boldness and witness to fall upon the Church. This was clearly a persistent theme in the early Church, for when they felt the boldness to witness slipping from them in the face of persecution, the people cried to God with great longing that that boldness should continue to rest upon them. We should do well to major on this theme in our revival praying.

Prayer for the unconverted

It is only a short step from praying for a spirit of witness to praying for those to whom the witness is to be made. It is the most natural of steps and doubtless one that the disciples took quickly during those ten days. They must have begun to pray for all sorts of people, Jew and Gentile alike. It is hard to say how full their hearts were with Jesus' compassion "for the crowds". No doubt that increased immeasurably as the Spirit fell on them later. But it is easy to imagine how, during those ten days, they must have been reminded of Jesus' great cry from the Cross, "Father forgive them, for they know not what they do". It might well have been a time when the Spirit brought back to them the love and compassion which Jesus had so obviously displayed for the ordinary run of people. At the same time, they may also have felt deeply convicted over their lack of those graces which were so evident in their Master, and so may have given themselves to earnest prayer that those graces should be more evident in their lives. It is certainly the case that such longing after love and grace is the very best way to open the gate to an inflow of the Spirit, who alone can supply such needs.

Intercession for people of all sorts, born of genuine love for them, is always at the heart of revival praying. Here, once again, a sanctified imagination allied to first-hand knowledge and understanding of people is highly important. The disciples had certainly mixed with every kind of person since they had followed Jesus, and they had acquired a remarkable window into humanity to help them pray.

As they thought and prayed over the crowds to whom

they were to witness, they could scarcely have been unmindful of the religious and political authorities, especially in Jerusalem. One important issue would have been thrown up as they prayed for these authorities, and indeed, as they prayed for the people of Jerusalem generally. Both authorities and people had been guilty of deliberately rejecting the salvation of God and of crucifying their Messiah. The disciples would need to confess this before God and earnestly implore Him to forgive their fellow countrymen. Jesus had clearly led the way in this sort of praying when on the Cross He had asked God to forgive His persecutors, or at least those among them who were acting ignorantly. "Father, forgive them, they know not what they do", had been His cry. Stephen was to do the same later as he was being stoned to death. His cry was, "Do not hold this sin against them," and that cry seems to have prevailed even for his chief persecutor, Saul of Tarsus. There seems little doubt that the disciples would have prayed in a similar way during those ten days.

Acknowledging and confessing the sins of those for whom one is praying is a thoroughly biblical activity, especially when it is accompanied by cries for God to have mercy on them. The prayers of Daniel and Nehemiah on behalf of their countrymen are another clear example of such intercession (Daniel 9:1ff and Nehemiah 1:4ff). It will always have a very important place in prayer for an outpouring of the Spirit. The reason for that is obvious — when we are seeking for such an outpouring we are seeking for widespread salvation amongst unbelievers, and not least amongst those who have wantonly sinned against God. A real grasp of the inevitability and horror of the judgement of God will spur us on to make confession for such people and to plead that God may have mercy on them.

It is important, however, that we are careful to notice that such prayer is confession. It is not, strictly speaking, repentance. We can confess to God the sin of another and admit his guilt and cry for mercy, but we cannot repent for another. Repentance is something that a person has to do for himself. It is a deliberate turning away from sin, and it cannot be done by proxy. A person may well turn to God as a result of our confession of his sin and our pleading for God's mercy, but it is he who must repent, when he accepts God and turns from his sinful behaviour.

Of course, there may well be moments when Christians must repent. They may need to repent of hard, dogmatic attitudes, or of prayerlessness, or of a failure to do the will of God. Christians may well find this necessity facing them as they seek to move closer to God and into revival. Such repentance will mean a deliberate change of direction, a deliberate renunciation of what has been wrong. It should be a definite, once-for-all act, however, and should be followed by a clear movement forward to grasp God's promises in faith. Continual repentance by Christians is not a healthy sign of real movement to holiness. A firm, definite act of repentance leading to a fundamental change of behaviour is far better.

That having been said, we should not in any way underestimate the importance of that deep heart-cry which springs out of a sense of brokenness over the sins which are being committed either by people at large or by the Church. Outpourings of the Spirit upon Church and nation alike may well call for protracted periods of such brokenness and confession. They may well mingle over a long period of time with strong affirmations of faith in God's promises to revive and to pour out His Spirit. The more one is involved in the process of seeking God for a visitation of His Spirit, the more one finds oneself in a movement which alternates from moments of high praise for His promises and His power to moments of deep confession and intercession. All the spiritual states within this movement are prompted by the Spirit and all have their place. It seems very much as though the early disciples tasted them all.

Notes

1. T. Shaw, Foreword to *Heaven Came Down* by John Weir, a contemporary account of the 1859 Revival in Ireland.
2. Rosalind Goforth, *Goforth of China*, pp. 177ff.
3. Marie Monsen, *The Awakening*, p. 28.
4. Ibid., p. 28.
5. See Chapter 2.
6. It is essential to keep in mind the fact that the history of revivals does not indicate that extensive preconditions have had to be fulfilled by large numbers of people in order for revival to take place. Quite the reverse. There seems to be no doubt that the crucial factor is a dedicated and thirsty group of believers who plead for a sheer intervention of the mercy of God towards what appears to be a godless and immoral society. See Chapter 3.

An individual may seek and obtain great spiritual help from God: and that is one thing. For a company *of people to unite to seek a new visitation from God is quite another thing, and is a spiritual labour greatly superior to the first.*

Historically, revivals have been mainly the achieving of a oneness of mind among a number of Christian believers.

A. W. Tozer

Chapter 6: Crucial Response (2)

They all joined together constantly . . .

Acts 1:14

When the day of Pentecost came, they were all together in one place.

Acts 2:1

The "hidden springs" of revival which give rise to the first trickles of Holy Spirit blessing invariably turn out to be periods of earnest prayer. As prayer increases, the trickles grow into broad streams, and where there are many springs and streams a river emerges. That is the way of revival. The river so formed will have many features, but it will always retain the character of the springs that gave it birth: it will always be a river of prayer. If the prayer dries up, invariably the river dries up too.

Obviously, the more converging streams and springs there are, the greater will be the river and the more powerful its effect. In plain terms, the width and power of any revival blessing will be directly related to the degree of unity in the Church. There will never be a really full and wide flow of the Spirit of God unless there is a uniting of the people of God. This is particularly the case in the matter of prayer. The greater the uniting in prayer, the greater the growth of the river.

The nature and power of united prayer

A very instructive example of one of these "hidden springs" was uncovered by Thomas Phillips, a contemporary witness to the revival which made a great impact on Wales in 1859. He relates that a certain Humphrey Jones, a Wesleyan preacher, had spent some time in the United States and "having witnessed much of the revival work in that country, was now anxious on his return to his native country to witness a similar outpouring of God's Holy Spirit there". He sought to rouse professing Christians to greater activity, including more earnest prayer, "maintaining that an *awakened church* is to be the principal instrument in converting the world". One of the persons he sought to rouse was a Calvinistic Methodist preacher named David Morgan. Jones suggested that they pray together, but his forthright invitation met with a negative response from Morgan. None the less, what Jones had said to him "had such a powerful influence on him that he could not sleep for several nights, but continued in earnest prayer for the guidance of the Spirit". Eventually, and with some reluctance, Morgan told Jones, "we cannot do much harm by keeping prayer meetings even if there be nothing but man in it after all". So they met for prayer. The following Sunday, after Jones had preached at one of his services, the Spirit moved so powerfully that every one of the whole congregation "put down his head and wept". Morgan was present, to see what happened, and he was immediately convinced that Jones' revival vision was right and that they should continue to meet for prayer.[1]

The sequel is interesting. Phillips continues his account: "the following week the two churches, Wesleyan and Calvinistic Methodists, united to keep prayer meetings every night alternately". He then reports that "old backsliders began to return. Men came in crowds from the mountains and all the country around until we were afraid the chapel would come down."[2] Small trickles were uniting and fast becoming a stream.

This episode illustrates very pointedly a number of important general characteristics of revival. First, it involved two completely unknown and, in the worldly sense, unimportant people. Secondly, the location was extremely remote and not at all famous. Thirdly, the source of the revival water was in the heart of a man who had discovered the flow of the Spirit while in another country. Fourthly, there was a willingness in his heart to go for the vision and go for it alone if necessary. Fifthly, he had difficulty in convincing others — at least initially. Features such as these are often to be found in revivals.

For our purposes in this chapter, however, two further features of this little cameo are particularly important. First of all, Jones was quite determined not merely to arouse others to pray for revival, but to arouse others who were not in any sense denominationally aligned to himself. Denominational difference was not a factor in his thinking. The only thing that mattered to him was to see God move in the power of the Spirit. When he sought out David Morgan he was actually seeking out someone from quite a different background. These two men belonged to two separate Methodist groups — the Wesleyans and the Calvinists — which in past history had divided with some bitterness. In fact it was that very same division which had caused such a sad rift between two of the greatest Christian leaders of the previous century, namely Whitefield and Wesley. Morgan followed Whitefield's Calvinism and Jones was happy to follow the more Arminian stance of Wesley. Perhaps Morgan's initial prejudice against Jones' exhortations that "something should be done" derived from his Calvinistic theological tradition. But the fact which stands out is that they worked through their differences because they were open for God to move in power. They both knew that this openness was of the utmost importance.

This historical example brings us face to face with the remarkable fact that whenever there is a true grasp of the vision of revival there is invariably a breaking free from narrow parochialism and from entrenched dogmatism. Exclusivism has never been a feature of revival. The breaking down of barriers, whether human or theological, is always amongst the first evidence that the hardness of the human heart is giving way and breaking up before a surge of the

Spirit. The more the Spirit flows, the more there is a readiness to fellowship with other believers — indeed, the more there is a recognition of the supreme importance of Jesus' desire that we "might be one". When the streams of revival flow there is never the slightest surrender of the great truth of the all-surpassing nature of Christ's substitutionary death on the Cross (nor of any other great Gospel truth), but neither is there any retreat into high-walled dogmatic castles from which stones are thrown at other believers, no matter what allegiance they may own. A heart of love and a readiness to cooperate are always present. Revival is a call to believers to be together where they may be together, not to be apart where they may differ. Those who have carried a burden for God to pour out His Spirit have always carried with them a desire to share that burden with others, no matter what their denominational roots have been. This has produced some extraordinary combinations at times, but also a remarkable fragrance too.

The second feature we should note is that the united prayers, which were first a feature of the fellowship of the two leaders and then a feature of their churches, were very powerful in their results. It was not just in answer to prayer that "men came in crowds from the mountains", but in answer to united prayer. An eyewitness of these united prayer meetings and the ensuing work of the Spirit said, "we soon had proof that the Lord was willing to accept our offerings, for there was a sweet-smelling flavour accompanying them".[2] The "sweet-smelling flavour" this eyewitness was referring to was the conversion of many people. This was indeed a sign that nothing is more acceptable to God than the offerings of united prayer.

A further example of the power of united prayer is provided for us by Phillips in the same book. He quotes a letter he received from a certain Rev T. L. Davies, a Baptist minister from Radnorshire, describing how revival began to move in his part of Wales:

That branch of the Church of Christ over which I preside

resolved to hold prayer meetings every night, to plead with the Lord for the outpouring of the Holy Spirit. These meetings were attended with unusual power. . . .

In the latter end of November it was proposed that we should hold *united prayer meetings*. This met with the hearty approval of all the dissenters in the town (Presteign), and the Baptists, Primitive Methodists, and the Wesleyans soon met successively at their respective chapels, without any semblance of sectarianism. All felt deeply the necessity of prayer – of united prayer and effort for the conversion of precious souls. . . .

This had a marked influence on the world; they saw that an earnest spirit of *united prayer* and *united effort* for their salvation prevailed. They saw that it was no longer the movement of a party or a sect. . . . Many now became deeply concerned about their souls, and earnestly sought the Lord for mercy.[3]

The sequence is interesting. First the Baptists met for earnest prayer. It then spread to the other denominations, and all began to meet together in rota at their respective churches. Finally the town began to feel the impact.

There can be no doubt, of course, that any individual church or grouping which earnestly seeks God's blessing in prayer will, quite certainly, see a move forward – even a touch of revival – as a result. But widespread blessing over whole cities or countries calls for a much wider basis of united prayer. It is important that we recognise that God has his eyes on our cities and that we are living in an age in which God is seeking to lift our horizons to widespread blessing. Moreover, we need further to recognise that we are being called to a full expression of united prayer activity in order that we may secure all that God is longing to give.

One of the greatest weaknesses the Christian Church is experiencing at the moment is the lack of true united and prolonged prayer for outpoured Holy Spirit blessing. The principle outlined above of different churches uniting to pray for their village and area is not a principle remote from us in our own generation. What was true of a village then is equally true of a large city today. The coming together of Christian people from different backgrounds in order to cry to God for widespread blessing is precisely what is required at this moment in our cities. In some ways the exercise may be rather more difficult by virtue of the size of modern cities, but the objective must be the same. One of the indicators that revival really is near will undoubtedly be a new release of widespread, united praying amongst what are now so many fragmented, not to say hostile, churches. When this begins to happen within our large conurbations we may expect to see some very widespread blessing and reaping.

It is an interesting fact that some of the most widespread blessing that has ever been seen in American and British cities occurred in 1859–60 when the "union prayer meeting" was at its height. In New York some 10,000 people were meeting daily for prayer, from every denomination. They had no hidden denominational agendas, but sought only the outpoured blessing of God. The same phenomenon was to be found in every town and city of the United States, and a truly national and city-wide movement of revival took place. When the revival movement crossed the Atlantic the same feature was quickly observed in Britain. In Belfast some 20,000 people gathered from all over Ireland for united prayer.[4] In London numerous and large prayer meetings were the order of the day. Needless to say, the revival made a tremendous impact on almost every major town in the country.

While it is true that such extraordinary united praying may be a sovereign work of the Spirit, it must also be something for which we need to gain a vision and to which we must begin to make a move.

One of the reasons , however, for looking into the relative obscurity of mid-nineteenth-century Welsh revival history in order to illustrate the prime importance of unity is to make clear the point that when the trickle of revival first begins to flow, it flows out of the hearts of obscure and ordinary ministers and people, who will take an initiative in their own area and follow the promptings of their own hearts without waiting for others. We need in our cities people who will do precisely that, and start to link up groups from different churches in united prayer for a moving of the Spirit. If it is not possible for this to take place across the denominational boundaries, then it needs to take place at the very least within denominations. Springs rise in the obscurity of the mountains, and revival springs must rise in seemingly obscure places, where people with vision begin to meet together for prayer. It is only out of such obscure beginnings that great rivers of revival have their source. It is impossible to overestimate the importance of such sources of united prayer.

For many, sadly, the starting-point will be not so much to achieve unity of prayer and direction with other churches as to achieve a unity within the local church itself. Perhaps the following illustration will provide comfort for any in such a position as well as reinforcing the general call to united action.

For at least a hundred years a small central European fellowship called the Moravian Church had a tremendous impact upon the development of modern missions. It was the Moravians who passed on the flame of fire to John Wesley for the revival of eighteenth-century Britain. However, at first this fellowship had a great problem with disunity. Before any living water could flow from the Moravians this great slab of spiritual concrete had to be broken. Unity was their greatest need.

The Moravians had some unpromising beginnings. Count Zinzendorf, their great founder and leader, had given refuge on his estates to many persecuted Christians from very varied backgrounds. They had formed a settlement called Herrnhut ("the Lord's Watch"). But the year 1727 saw Zinzendorf, a great man of prayer, confronted with the problem of "how to unite in faith and love and service the pious but disputatious followers of Huss, Luther, Calvin, Zwingli, Schweckfeld, etc., etc. . . . it seemed a hopeless problem apart from prayer . . . questions of predestination, holiness, the meaning and mode of baptism etc., etc., seemed likely to divide the believers into a number of small and belligerent sects. . . . Then the more earnest and spiritual souls among them began to cry out for deliverance."[5]

Zinzendorf, earnestly looking for an intervention from God, drew up a "Brotherly Covenant" which called upon them to "seek out and emphasise the points on which they agreed" rather than to stress their differences. It also called them to a solemn covenant of renewed dedication of their lives to the service of the Lord Jesus Christ.

God worked and a new spirit began to be felt. In the considered opinion of a Moravian bishop, this process "made possible . . . the frequent gathering of bands for prayer that next marked the ensuing months and led the way to and prepared for the baptism of the Spirit that culminated on that 'blessed 13th of August' ".[6] The date he referred to was the occasion when the Moravians, gathered together for a Communion service, received a tremendous revelation of the Calvary love of Jesus and were baptised with a Spirit of supplication and mutual love. It was out of that renewed love in the Church that the extraordinary flow of prayer, revival and missionary endeavour sprang.

There can be no doubt, therefore, that unity within groupings and between groupings is a cardinal secret of the prayer that prevails for the outpouring of the Spirit. It is not something that will come automatically but is something to work for. It is one of those vital preparations that precede revival. We need to take very much to heart the kind of determination to secure a real unity that Zinzendorf exemplified.

The call to unity

Biblically there can be no mistaking the crucial importance of unity as far as seeking for Holy Spirit blessing is concerned. Psalm 133 in particular, though short, is a devastatingly clear demand for such unity. The first verse of that Psalm tells us that unity is pleasant to God, but the last verse tells us that it is when brothers live in unity that God actually commands His blessings. We have to remember that simple fact — that all blessings are commanded by God. They are not ordered by us or arranged by our planning. And the order for blessing goes out from God when we are united. More than this, we need to note that such unity is depicted in this Psalm as being like the oil on Aaron's beard and the dew on Hermon. Both of these pictures are symbolic of the Holy Spirit. In other words, a readiness to unite is in some sense tantamount to a flow of the Holy Spirit. If our hearts are longing for an outpouring of the Spirit of God, then they must join together in unity, which is the only channel along which a greater and fuller flow of the Spirit may come.

This same truth is, of course, very evident in the praying which led up to the outpouring of the Spirit on the Day of Pentecost. Luke tells us that they prayed "with one mind" (Acts 1:14). The word used here (*homothumadon*) appears ten times in Acts, and each time it indicates a powerful unity of direction which springs from complete agreement of mind. Obviously they had no denominational barriers to overcome, but they had their personality differences and they certainly had their quarrels over who was most important. Perhaps we need to remember that so-called denominational and theological barriers are frequently far less rooted in the defence of the truth than in pride, personality and emotional instability. It is generally the case that harmful division is removed not so much by the reconciliation of different views of truth as by the confession of dogmatism, pride and hardness of heart. The Cross is the place of reconciliation, and the Cross calls for a flow of love, forgiveness, acceptance and co-operation.

As we shall see later, unity in the Body of Christ as a result of the outpouring of the love of the Spirit is one of the most marked features of true revival. If we are praying for revival blessing, we have no alternative but to seek to walk this pathway of unity. It is absurd even to think of praying for the Spirit and for revival if we are not going to open ourselves to unity.

101

Of course, we cannot wait for total unity before pressing on to pray for revival blessing. A. W. Tozer offers some practical advice here:

> Unity embracing one hundred per cent of the people is not required before God begins to work. God responds to even "two or three" who may be gathered in His name; the extent and power of His working will depend upon the size of the nucleus with relation to the total number of believers within the church.[7]

Addressing the problem of doctrinal differences, he writes:

> Revival unity is not the same as doctrinal unity. God demands no more than oneness in *all things that matter*; in all others things we are free to think as we will. The disciples at Pentecost were one only in the things of the Spirit; in everything else they were one hundred and twenty. Harmony may be defined as oneness at points of contact. It need extend no further than this to meet the requirements of revival. God will bless a body of men and women who are one in spiritual purpose, even if their doctrinal positions are not identical on every point.[8]

There must, then, be a readiness immediately to seek God for revival whenever a union of heart and intent is discovered, even though only a few may be involved. But at the same time there must be a diligent seeking of other revival-minded believers, whatever background they may come from.

Unity amongst leaders — a crucial factor

There is a further and extremely important aspect to united praying which is clearly brought out in Acts. This has to do with the role of those in leadership. When we read carefully the text of Acts we notice that the prayer response which took place in the upper room involved in the first instance the apostles, "the women" and Jesus' mother and brothers. This means that the leaders and their closest supporters were together in the forefront of the prayer. No doubt the rest of the one hundred and twenty were soon involved, but the pace was set by the apostles and those closest to them.

This praying together was something that characterised the apostles' ministry. The expression in Acts 6:4, "we will give ourselves to prayer", has an unmistakably corporate side to it. It was a practice picked up by the second generation of leaders, some of whom we see waiting on God together in Antioch (Acts 13:1−2). There was regularity in such meetings, there was commitment and there was very obviously much power. It was the place where the Spirit was abroad. Quite simply we have in Acts a picture of united prayer in which leadership took a very clear and committed role. It was not left to the followers, and that is undoubtedly why it had such a deep and powerful impact. Leaders need to pray and to unite in prayer. When both factors operate widespread blessing is assured.

Let us return for a moment to our initial illustration from the Welsh revival of 1860. Perhaps one of the most challenging aspects of that episode lies not simply in the fact that Calvinists and Wesleyans actually met for prayer, but that the two respective ministers were themselves deeply involved in the process. The attempt by the one to seek out his fellow minister and express to him the depth of burden that was on his heart was a move of the utmost importance. Here was no formalised nod in the direction of fellowship, but a deep desire for the genuine sharing of a heart-concern. There was no "hidden agenda", denominationally or otherwise, with Humphrey Jones. There was only a burning desire to see an outpouring of the Spirit for the glory of Jesus. His heart longed for the Kingdom before all else. If he had any misgivings about his colleague's Calvinism he was not going to let them stand in the way of searching him out for fellowship. Perhaps the dogmatisms which in an earlier generation might have kept both these men brittle and apart had, mercifully, mellowed sufficiently to enable them to have meaningful fellowship for the sake of the work of Jesus. Difficult though it may have been initially, they were prepared to talk together, pray together and work together. At that point blessing came. It is because this point is not always reached by ministers and leaders that so much promised blessing never actually comes.

It seems to me impossible to overestimate the importance of a coming together of those who are in leadership in different groupings within the Church for the purpose of earnestly seeking God for an outpouring of the Holy Spirit. The reason why it is so important is simply that in doing this the leaders reveal a selfless desire that God's blessing should not be confined to their own areas of responsibility or their own churches. It shows that humility and largeness of heart which earnestly want a fellow minister's work to be blessed and successful. It shows that the leaders' fears and insecurities have been cast out in a genuine flow of love. All this inevitably brings a wealth of blessing from God. If leaders are prepared for a genuine exercise of such prayer-fellowship, then there will be ripples of enormous consequence in their congregations. "Like pastor like people" is as true here as anywhere: what the leaders are, the congregations will become. Here is the secret of deep and widespread blessing.

We need to take note of the fact that suspicion, fear, dogmatism and party spirit most certainly quench the Spirit of God. Undoubtedly this, together with a lack of prayerfulness, is the greatest obstacle to Holy Spirit blessing. This attitude cannot be avoided in a passive way — it can only be avoided by positive activity in the opposite direction. There really isn't any "no man's land" here! Here leadership must lead. We must disregard those who cry, "That's too simplistic!"

The prayer which spreads

We can further underline the importance of response among leaders to united praying by indicating the principle by which a spirit of prayer actually grows. The principle is simply this: when there is a true union of prayer in a nucleus group, and that prayer is directed toward widespread spiritual blessing, invariably that same spirit of prayer begins to make itself felt in widening circles. Earnest prayer creates room for the Spirit of God to impress others with a desire to pray. Prayer is a fire which catches, a stream which cuts deeper and deeper — but it needs a starting-point. Prayer is a multiplying phenomenon which begins not so much through talk and exhortation (though that has its place) as through people actually praying. It certainly can be taught, but it is most often caught.

This ripple or knock-on effect of the spirit of prayer is very clearly illustrated in Colin Whittaker's book *Prayer Mountains*. He describes how the extraordinary intercessory prayer-flow of the Korean revivals has found a focus in the phenomenon of prayer mountains. The most powerful of these prayer retreats sees some thousands praying and fasting daily for every kind of need. The origin of this phenomenon is not to be found in a committee plan or even in a godly idea. It is to be found in the activity of a woman who gave herself to praying for long periods upon a mountain and whose ministry God Himself multiplied ten thousandfold. This woman (Dr Jashil Choi) at first made do with a tent, and every night for three years she was there praying until the first sanctuary on the site was opened in July 1974. A simple beginning, with one praying woman, has developed into a place where there are prayer meetings every day of the year. Great numbers of people go there with one purpose — to pray.[9]

It is worth noting here that the extraordinary and gigantic river of daily prayer which flows in the Korean church has a faraway source in the extremely dedicated prayer among missionaries and Korean church leaders at the turn of the century. Often stimulated by persecution, that prayer has never died out, and indeed has multiplied beyond recognition. It is one of the greatest challenges to come to the Western church. It clearly demonstrates the principle of the leavening process of prayer.

Zinzendorf's life is a tremendous challenge to prospective leaders. He learned the secret of prevailing prayer early in life. By the time he left college at the age of sixteen he had founded "seven praying societies". He prayed for the warring members of the Moravian fellowship until they themselves were meeting together for prayer. He prayed with tears for a small group of young girls to be really touched by God, and as a result great intercession poured out of the lips of the Moravian children. Small wonder that the time immediately prior to the outpouring at Herrnhut was characterised by an extraordinary spirit of prayer, and that the outpouring itself produced an unparalleled spirit of supplication.

Some of the most edifying and uplifting prayer sessions I have been privileged to attend occurred at the Prayer and Bible Weeks introduced by Denis Clark. The three ingredients of worship, Word and intercession were woven together in a tremendously powerful spiritual cord. There was a distinct fragrance abroad. I learned that these times had begun with Denis Clark setting aside the opening week of a particular year and waiting upon God by himself in precisely this way. The following year others of like mind joined him. First the numbers were small, but they grew and grew as the years went by. Eventually so many wished to be involved that the Prayer and Bible Weeks had to be held in the Swanwick Conference Centre. They were so much more than mere conferences: they grew out of a true spirit of prayer and love of the Word, and they breathed that spirit. Eventually similar conferences were organised especially for ministers and leaders. It is a brave man who calls ministers together not to talk and plan but rather to pray at length and to expose themselves to the Word, but there is nothing so vital as that. Needless to say, the spiritual ripples from those Prayer and Bible Weeks were very significant indeed.

Real prayer multiplies prayer. Leadership must never opt out of the challenge of this. Ministers may not necessarily be called to a ministry of intercession as deep as that which is laid upon some of their people, but waiting upon God must be their top priority if it is to feature in their people. The surest way to powerful united prayer among Christians is that of united prayer among their leaders.

We conclude with a final illustration from the 1858 revival in the United States. Edwin Orr notes that one of the sources of that great outpouring was a convention in Pittsburgh attended by Presbyterian ministers from several cities. It was called in response to news of revival outbreaks in Canada. Orr describes it as follows:

> The convention continued in session for three days, considering the necessity of a general revival of religion in the churches represented and in others as well. Agenda of the meetings included discussion of the means, the encouragements, and the hindrances, the demands of the times, the indications of divine providence and all related questions on revival.
>
> It was a solemn, anxious, melting and encouraging meeting. Two hundred ministers and many laymen attended, *and much of the time was spent in prayer* [my italics].

The ministers went back from that convention to preach on revival and to set up meetings for prayer. Very soon other denominational churches were doing the same. Within months revival had broken out.

That is where we must arrive if we are to see similar outpourings — at the place of united heart-searching and prayer after the widest blessing God can give.

Notes

1. Thomas Phillips, *The Welsh Revival*, pp. 7ff. This is a first-hand contemporary account.
2. Ibid., p. 9.
3. Ibid., p. 40.
4. Edwin Orr, *The Second Evangelical Awakening*, p. 47.

5. J. Greenfield, *Power from on High*, p. 22.
6. Ibid., p. 22.
7. A. W. Tozer, *Paths to Power*, p. 59.
8. Ibid., p. 59.
9. Colin Whittaker, *Korea Miracle*, pp. 123ff.

I set apart this day for prayer to God, and spent most of the day in that duty.

David Brainerd's Diary

Chapter 7: Crucial Response (3)

All these . . . devoted themselves to prayer.

Acts 1:14 (RSV)

But we will devote ourselves to prayer . . .

Acts 6:4 (RSV)

The challenge of the extraordinary

The description of the disciples prayer response in Acts 1:14 contains a third challenge to any serious prayer for revival. We are told that prayer was something to which *"they devoted themselves"*.

The Greek word used here means literally "to be strong in the direction of". It denotes an endurance, a steadfastness, a perseverance, a complete application to the work in hand, a determined attitude to get on with the business. It is a word used more than once by Luke. It describes the attitude of the believers towards the teaching they were receiving from the apostles in the Temple (Acts 2:42). It also describes the attitude of the apostles themselves towards their work of prayer and preaching (6:4). In both these instances it speaks of persistence and diligence, of commitment and consistency.

It was this determined attitude that took the disciples through what can be properly described only as a period of extraordinary prayer — extraordinary both in its extent and in its depth. Such prayer, of course, presents us immediately with a challenge. It shows us the level of prayer that is the forerunner of revival blessing. Not only do we need to be united in faith for the blessing of the Spirit, but we need to be in the presence of God in a very determined and, very

111

often, prolonged manner. If the history of revivals has anything to teach us, it is this.

Prayer has everything to do with faith and earnestness of heart. Very often we are surprised at the speed with which some answers seem to come — almost before we have asked! But no one can have engaged much in prayer without coming to realise how important time and persistence are to the whole process. Pious and empty repetition, devoid of real intent, has no place in true prayer. When we pray we want to secure things from God! But there will be many a time when prolonged prayer will be the only thing that secures an answer. Jesus himself emphasised the point on more than one occasion. The simple fact is that when we come to pray for great blessing, there is so much ground to cover in prayer, so much we need to hear from God. It cannot be done in a few brief minutes.

Extraordinary prayer — that is the calling and the aiming-point for those who would pray for powerful movements of God's Spirit. People's reluctance to engage in extraordinary prayer seems to be one of the most difficult of the obstacles which have to be overcome before any move towards deeper blessing can be initiated. There seems to be so often an inbuilt resistance to giving the best of our time to seeking God. Perhaps of all the things we need from God, the one we need the most is that quickening of spirit whereby we are released into determined application to prayer. It is a healthy sign in the Church when what is normally considered "extraordinary" comes to be seen as rather more "ordinary".

John Wesley's Journal contains a most striking entry for the New Year's Day of 1739, which was a few months after his conversion. It referred to a Moravian Love Feast in which some sixty Moravians and seven of the Oxford Methodists met to pray, sing psalms and give thanks. Charles Wesley and George Whitefield were among them. Wesley writes, "about three in the morning, as we were continuing instant in prayer, the power of God came mightily upon us, insomuch that many cried for exceeding joy, and many fell to the ground. As soon as we recovered a little from the awe and amazement at the presence of His majesty, we broke out with one voice — 'We praise Thee, O God; we acknowledge Thee to be the Lord!'"[1]

The challenge of that entry lies in the expression, "about three in the morning". That united group, Moravian and Anglican, had set out to spend the whole night before God, thinking such activity to be the best way of finishing one year and ushering in the next. God brought down a tremendous anointing upon them in the early hours. It could have come at the beginning, but in fact it did not. It came after several hours. How much they would have missed had they finished at midnight! And at three in the morning they did not want to finish!

Such activity was characteristic of the Moravians. They would spend many hours in prayer and singing of psalms. They did this before the great outpouring of the Spirit at Herrnhut, and afterwards they did it even more. From the earliest moments of that outpouring they organised themselves into programmes for round-the-clock praying for missionary work. Extraordinary praying was ordinary for them. Often demanding, it was none the less a delight. The Wesleys and Whitefield were swept into the flow of such prayer, with great results for Britain.

R. B. Jones, a prominent leader in the Welsh revival of 1904, provides another vivid example of extraordinary praying in his book, *Rent Heavens*. He includes in it a letter from a pastor which tells how revival broke out in his church. The pastor writes of the cold indifference that had characterised his people and then goes on:

However, one evening in the spring of 1903, some of our young brethren — four in number — were found on the mountain holding a meeting for prayer, and it transpired that they had been doing so every night for some months. Their one object was to pray for Revival. The brother who discovered them heartily joined them. When the news leaked out the whole church was moved by the thought

113

that her condition was so keenly felt by those who were so young . . . the praying on the mountain continued and those attending increased in number; even those who never entered a place of worship were attracted and remained to pray. As the numbers increased, so did the fervour. Presently, the flame reached the whole church, and we were moved with the Spirit of prayer and with a passion for souls. In an incredibly short time the whole neighbourhood was ablaze with the divine fire.[2]

Our problem, confronting the prospect of extraordinary prayer from the level of the ordinary, is that we see the extraordinary as some exceedingly high mountain, and our hearts and our bodies simply seem to melt into weakness before a nigh impossibility. We are left wondering whatever we would do with any protracted period of time. How would it be filled up? Equally, we tend to think immediately that it would be far too much to expect other people to respond to such a prayer onslaught. We are immensely thrilled by the stories of those who have scaled such heights and have seen such glorious vistas, but we are daunted by them and feel unable to do more than read them in armchair comfort. Yet we feel none the less that we are called to be strong, to do exploits, to attempt great things for God, to tread where others of "like passions" have trod. There must be many who feel such a tension.

Moving into extraordinary prayer

There are two things that we need to have quite clear in our minds when we face the challenge of extraordinary prayer. The first is that we must learn to bring the Spirit of God into our reckoning, and the second is that any programme we launch into must not be physically unrealistic. If we keep these in mind we will actually begin to scale the heights.

To take the second point first, we need to keep in mind that the Spirit of God does not operate generally by making unrealistic demands on us. He may make demands we may not like, and on occasions He may energise us to fulfil unusual demands, but He knows humanity's limitations. We cannot spend whole nights in prayer too frequently, we cannot fast continuously, we cannot start every day with a very early morning prayer meeting. That sort of prospect is certain to depress any would-be climbers. What we have to remember is that amazing things may be achieved if we periodically resort to these times of extraordinary prayer. The prayer which has ushered in revivals has been extraordinary, but also sensible and balanced. It is important to take note of this when planning extraordinary prayer.

Most important, however, is the fact that we have to learn to bring the Holy Spirit into our reckoning. What we sometimes fail to understand is that times of prayer such as those of Wesley and the Welsh youths do not spring totally out of human desire, nor are they sustained by human endeavour alone. They are due in large measure to the inspiration and energising of the Holy Spirit. This is no mere pious statement. It is actually true. The Holy Spirit is a great motivator, and it is precisely His work to touch our desires and fill our hearts with an increased appetite to pray. He is also the supreme energiser, enabling us to continue when humanly we would flag. Moreover, He is the great source of inspiration for specific praise and petition, and can constantly restock our minds as we pray. Anyone who has walked in the realm of prayer and has learned to walk in it with the Spirit will know the truth of this.

Andrew Murray makes some pertinent remarks in this connection. He reminds us that "this Holy Spirit is, in the first place, a Spirit of prayer. He was promised as a 'Spirit of grace and supplication'." He continues:

Deep in the inmost recesses of his being, hidden and unfelt, every child of God has the Holy, Mighty Spirit of God dwelling in him . . . As long as we measure our power for praying aright and perseveringly, by what we feel or think we can accomplish, we shall be discouraged when we hear of how much we ought to pray. But when

115

we believe that, in the midst of all our conscious weakness, the Holy Spirit as a Spirit of supplication is dwelling within us, *for the very purpose of enabling us to pray in such manner and measure as God would have us*, our hearts will be filled with hope. We shall begin to lose our sense of burden and fear and discouragement about our ever praying sufficiently, because we see that the Holy Spirit Himself will pray, is praying, in us.[3]

In other words, we are being called quite simply to exercise faith that the presence of the Holy Spirit will enter fully into our extraordinary times of prayer. This really is the secret of fruitful, prolonged and joyful prayer. In another passage Murray puts it like this: "Is it not clear that everything in prayer depends upon our trusting the Holy Spirit to do His work in us: yielding ourselves to His leading, depending only and wholly on Him?"

Not only is there a divine sustaining by the Spirit, but when we are moving in the flow of that Spirit the times of sustained prayer can actually become times of tremendous delight and joy. For the Spirit is never, of course, just calling us to doleful hard work — He is a Spirit of joy and delight. Once that delight is released into the work, the prayer meetings become a great source of increasing strength.

This is a truth which is wonderfully illustrated in the reflections of J. G. Govan, the founder of the Faith Mission. This great work of God, which has produced many a powerful evangelist for Scotland, began in the 1880s at the Water Street Mission Church in Glasgow. Reflecting on the early years that saw it gradually coming to birth, Govan wrote:

On looking back, there is one thing that stands out clearly in my mind, and that is the amount of time we gave to prayer. Prayer became a great joy. We delighted in it. The light of God's countenance and the atmosphere of praise and victory were most refreshing. Whole nights of prayer were then our experience, and many of our Saturday afternoons were given to prayer.[4]

To read through the accounts of those early days at the Water Street Mission is indeed to breathe a spirit of prayer. That was the soil in which the Faith Mission grew. Powerful works for God have never had any other soil! But there was joy in it, delight in it! They were times when Govan and his friends met the energising and directing power of the Holy Spirit, and cold formalism evaporated. There was "an atmosphere of praise and victory", and there is nothing more joyful than that.

Govan described one such occasion in more detail:

One Saturday night at Water Street we arranged to have a night of prayer, and had a wonderful outpouring of God's Holy Spirit. We commenced at ten o'clock, and we went on till six in the morning. We could not stop then, but went home for some breakfast and back again, continuing till midday. We had a wonderful time – a glorious time, a Hallelujah time. People say, "How could you go on so long?" But when the Spirit of God is outpoured, there is nothing difficult or hard about prayer.[5]

The secret of sustained and extraordinary prayer is very clearly indicated here. It is simply the presence of the Spirit Himself. Of course, in the case of this particular prayer meeting there was obviously quite an unusual manifestation of the Spirit, but unusual manifestations are not essential to that unmistakable energising and guiding ministry which the Spirit exercises (or can exercise, if we allow Him to) when we seek God in prayer.

Govan himself once expressed this same truth in robust manner:

My friends, get into this position of entire surrender to God, and real trust in Him, and then he will show you

117

when to wait on Him and how long to wait on Him; and He will visit you and bless you in a way perhaps you have little idea of now.

We should not imagine, of course, that moving with the Holy Spirit will be a constant "Hallelujah time". When the Spirit is moving the mood will change, and sometimes quite abruptly. We might well find the Spirit releasing great longings of heart. David Brainerd's heart-cries for the North American Indians epitomise this sort of praying. His diary records them, and amongst its entries we frequently read statements like this:

> In prayer I was exceedingly enlarged, and my soul was drawn out as ever I remember it to have been in my life. I was in such anguish and pleaded with such earnestness that when I arose from my knees I could scarcely walk straight.[6]

We need to acknowledge at once that if this kind of note is not struck in our extraordinary praying, then something is very seriously amiss, just as we need to acknowledge that absence of "Hallelujahs" would also indicate that something was amiss. Strong, powerful praise, mingling with deeper, quieter worship, moving on to earnest petition and strong cries — all prompted by the Spirit — is the stuff of which extraordinary prayer is made.

We should not imagine either that the energising of the Spirit will remove from us the sheer slog of a deliberate and determined attitude to do business with God. The Spirit will give us grit to go on when things are not very exciting, and when we are working at prayer because we know that this is the King's business which we must get on with. There are not many nights of prayer that do not include times like that. However, one must hasten to add that we should not assume that such prayer nights will consist entirely of hard work.

Extraordinary prayer — the herald of revival

The sure and certain mark of an approaching outpouring of the Spirit has always been the emergence of this kind of prayer. No revival has come without it, and when it begins to appear on a wide front, without any obvious human prompting, we can be sure we are hearing "the sound of wind in the mulberry trees". When revival is about to break out, this kind of earnest, extraordinary prayer can pour out like a huge cataract as the Spirit floods into the hearts of God's people.

Perhaps one of the most outstanding and well-known examples of this was to be seen in the middle years of the last century in America. In September 1857, a Dutch Reformed city missioner called a prayer meeting in downtown New York. Within six months, ten thousand businessmen were meeting for prayer daily in that city. Tremendous eagerness and concern for the lost was expressed. Tens of thousands were converted. It was a flood of prayer which flowed through thousands of towns in the States. But it did not happen simply because a prayer meeting was called. It happened because the Spirit of God began to commandeer the hearts of thousands of Christian people and cause them to cry to God in a way that only He could. Wherever the flood of prayer went, a flood of conversions followed. The Holy Spirit was being manifested as a spirit of supplication and conviction.[7]

This was a remarkable example of the gushing out of the Spirit of supplication — a kind of miracle of prayer. We have to remember, however, that the same sort of powerful stirrings to prayer may come in a far less obvious and startling manner, and yet have equally widespread results. We do not always need to be moving in the realm of the spectacular in order to see God at work. The following accounts may help us to recognise this and strengthen us to press on with those promptings which the Spirit is giving us.

The first concerns the awakening in Wales in 1904 and the revivals which were its counterparts in other parts of the world. Jessie Penn Lewis was much involved in the Welsh awakening, and was also conversant with the other wider movements of the Spirit. Looking for the first stirrings of all these awakenings, she observed that they were preceded by a fairly long and ever-increasing burden of prayer, spread throughout all the areas that were eventually touched by the Spirit.[8]

She noted, for example, that in the Moody Bible Institute in the late 1890s there were "three to four hundred children of God meeting every Saturday night to pray for a 'worldwide Revival'". She noted also that "After a time a few began to stay in prayer late at night, and ceased not until the early hours of the Sabbath morning."

She reported that in Melbourne, Australia, "forty thousand praying souls meet in two thousand homes encircling the city in prayer, and many met for half nights of prayer". In India "the Divine Spirit laid the same burden upon the servants of God, and guided them, without any conscious connection with the prayer movements in other lands, to form an all-India prayer circle of those who would unite to plead for the outpoured Spirit upon that dark and needy land". One of the "other lands" so mentioned was Britain, where prayer circles mushroomed rapidly in 1902.

Returning to her native Wales she found streams that had flowed almost unnoticed for a very long time: "we go to the Rhondda Valley, where afterwards the Spirit of God swept with such power, and hear of some who for years had been pleading for a Revival which should 'sweep over the whole world'".

This background to those revivals of the first decade of the twentieth century will be well known to the explorers of the beginnings of revival. However, there is another, more recent period which has not been so well explored, and which is yet of particular interest for our present situation.[9] The period I am referring to is the 1950s in Britain. The more one looks into that decade, the more it becomes evident that it was a remarkable time of extraordinary prayer, with some far-reaching results.

A good starting-point from which to explore this decade is the Billy Graham Crusade at Harringay in 1954. By any account that was a very powerful crusade, producing not only large numbers of converts but also many future full-time Christian workers in all fields. At the back of that crusade were nights of prayer. When the crusade was over these were continued, at first for the purpose of praying for Billy Graham and his further crusades, and then, at the suggestion of George Ingram, a retired missionary, for the purpose of praying for worldwide revival. These nights of prayer were held each month until well into the 1960s. Significantly, the night of prayer in London began to have offshoots in many parts of the country, until they were to be found in "scores of towns".[10] It was a phenomenon also, I believe, amongst many unknown, smaller groups who remained unlinked to the London meeting.

This was not, however, the only such stream of prayer for revival that began to flow through the country at that time, though possibly it was the most obvious and widespread. The 1950s were a decade in which some powerful injections of the revival vision were given to the churches by some leading preachers, injections which were accompanied by very powerful calls to prayer. In the fifties Christians were still tuned in to the Hebridean revival of 1949, and they began to gain a consciousness that 1959 was the centenary year of the great 1859 revival in America and Great Britain. In 1956 Arthur Wallis, moved by the Hebridean revival, wrote his much-acclaimed book, *In the Day of Thy Power*. In 1958 Arthur Skevington Wood published a collection of his sermons and articles on revival, and throughout the whole of 1959. Martyn Lloyd-Jones preached on this same subject. Doctor W. E. Sangster gave his final address at the Methodist Conference in 1958, and of that occasion Roy Pointer writes: "he knew that all revivals had been preceded and accompanied by prayer, and he called Methodism to passionate pleading and persistent prayer for revival. Doctor Sangster was concerned for the plight of the nation and the role of his own denomination".[11]

There were a great number of remarkable experiences of the Spirit of prayer abroad in those days. One of these comes from the personal diary of a Christian Literature Crusade missionary. She writes that when the manuscript for Arthur Wallis' book on revival reached the CLC for publication, it became the subject of unusual and earnest prayer among members of that mission. Along with others, she prayed much that it would be a book greatly used by God. She was in point of fact one of the workers assigned to read the manuscript, and she describes in detail what happened as her work on the book progressed:

> As I read the manuscript it had the effect of confronting me with "the word of the Lord" and demanding an answer. I gave it. And so on behalf of several others, I asked permission to ask members of the Crusade to an early morning prayer meeting each day to pray only for Revival. These times of prayer continued daily for many weeks and finally led up to the week of the Annual Conference.
>
> The visiting speaker knew nothing of our times of prayer and heart searching. But he came straight from a time of revival in the Belgian Congo [now Zaire]. We began with a season of prayer but not for the Agenda. The Spirit of God led away from business matters altogether. I well remember how one after another rose to their feet to pray, how there was such contrition, such confession of sin . . . At once we knew we were in the Presence of a Holy God. Others in the room were forgotten except when help was needed. And then the combined praises made us realize the strength and power and sympathy of such a fellowship. Revival had come.
>
> No agenda was used that day or any day of the whole Conference. The visitation of God continued each and all day long.

At the end of the Conference on the last morning 14 people were healed. As each came from the healing place we sang spontaneously "O the cleansing Blood has reached me, Glory, Glory to the Lamb!"

Following this glorious week we went back to our shops and offices. That year there was not a single CLC Centre where people were not being converted to God. Not only in the Centres but wherever members of that Conference were, unbelievers came to God. It was a glorious year.[12]

The 1950s produced many testimonies of this kind. In this decade Christians had a remarkable grip on revival vision and the Spirit of prayer was unleashed in a powerful way.

Where did all this prayer lead? There were certain powerful movings of the Spirit, such as that experienced by the CLC workers, but, of course, there was no real national awakening. What we do have to register, however, even though it still may not be palatable to all, is that God began to bring a very powerful new experience of the Holy Spirit into the lives of many leaders and many congregations. It was a movement in which thousands came to a new experience of the power and fullness of the Holy Spirit, the importance of which we shall consider in the next chapter.

Starting as a trickle in the fifties and involving such people as Arthur Wallis, Denis Clark and Campbell MacAlpine, it gathered momentum until by the early sixties it began to escalate rapidly. It penetrated all the main denominations. Among the Anglicans, Michael Harper (one of George Ingram's prayer targets!), David Watson, David MacInness and John Gunstone, to name but a few, experienced a new surge of Holy Spirit life that became the basis for widespread and long-lasting ministries. From the sixties the flow continued into the seventies. It was still pulsating in the eighties and by that time some very powerful "House Church" ministries had emerged and real rapprochement with the Pentecostal churches had become evident. Without any question new life had swept into the Church.

In relating the praying of the fifties to the movement of

the Holy Spirit in the three decades which followed, Peter Hocken has made some extremely pertinent comments. He writes:

> It is evident from the accounts recorded that circles of evangelical Christians praying for revival were among those most affected by the early occurrences of charismatic blessing . . . Concern and prayer for revival were evidently a form of preparation for pentecostal blessing. This concern and prayer itself intensified desire for revival and increased the intercessors' openness to receive the forms of revival that God might send.[13]

It seems indisputable that there has been a very direct connection between the revival vision and extended prayer of the fifties and the following three decades of Holy Spirit quickening in the ministries of thousands of leaders and many more thousands of churchgoers. It is precisely the kind of connection that we are accustomed to seeing in many previous historic movements of God. The praying was prompted by the Holy Spirit, it was extraordinary and it was fuelled by powerful preaching; there were moments when the Spirit moved with extraordinary manifestations on certain groups; and people spent whole days and nights in prayer making a "business of it".

So can we call what happened in the sixties, seventies and eighties revival? Almost without exception the answer must be No. There is something more to be seen before that term becomes applicable. But among those involved in the renewal of the last three decades is the feeling that it was very much a part of the process of revival and may well yet be proved to have been an essential basis for a full revival outpouring in the future. Renewal may not be revival, but its characteristics are undoubtedly part of the apostolic pattern or blueprint.

All of this must encourage us to set our sails to catch the wind of the Spirit of supplication. We need to be ready and moving into realms of prayer that are beyond our normal experience. Such praying is never without its reward. If we have to wait many years for the full expression of the answers to such prayers, so be it. It is what we have been called to. We need to respond.

Notes

1. John Wesley, *Journal*.
2. R. B. Jones, *Rent Heavens*, p. 34f.
3. Andrew Murray, *Ministry of Intercession*, p. 118.
4. I. R. Govan, *Spirit of Revival*, p. 26.
5. Ibid., p. 26.
6. Ibid., p. 27.
7. Many such examples are selected by Oswald J. Smith in his *The Lives of Brainerd and Fletcher*.
8. Jessie Penn Lewis, *The Awakening in Wales*, ch. 1.
9. Peter Hocken's *Streams of Renewal* is a very valuable exploration of these years.
10. Edward England, Foreword to the commemorative edition of Arthur Wallis, *In the Day of Thy Power*.
11. R. Pointer, *How do Churches Grow?*, p. 38.
12. A personal testimony written for the author, 1989.
13. Peter Hocken, op. cit., p. 157.

But for the Spirit's special enduement that came upon me during a crisis in my life as a missionary, I would have been compelled to abandon the field and return home as a failure.

Pilkington of Uganda

Today the Holy Ghost is as truly available and as mighty in power as He was on the Day of Pentecost . . . our desperate need today is for a fresh enduement of power.

Hudson Taylor

I believe there is a Pentecostal blessing to be received: the anointing of the Holy Spirit and enduement with power.

Andrew Murray

I have asked God if there were ever a day when I should stand in the pulpit and preach without compassion and fire, I want God to take me home to heaven. I don't want to live. I don't ever want to stand in the pulpit and preach without the power of the Holy Spirit. It's a dangerous thing.

Billy Graham

Chapter 8: Baptised in the Spirit (1)

. . . before many days you shall be baptised with the Holy Spirit . . .

Acts 1:5

When the day of Pentecost had come they were all filled with the Holy Spirit.

Acts 2:4

It was Jesus who promised the Spirit and it was Jesus who poured out the Spirit. "Exalted to the right hand of God, he has received from the Father the promised Holy Spirit and has poured out what you now see and hear." That was what Peter declared to the assembled crowds on the Day of Pentecost (Acts 2:33).

One hundred and twenty people received that initial outpouring, and it radically changed them and equipped them for all that lay ahead of them. They began to glorify God as a new spirit of praise and faith rose up from within them. Peter launched forth with a new boldness and liberty to proclaim to the crowds the resurrection of the Lord. A great sense of oneness and commitment bound the disciples together even more than before, and, witnessing with great eagerness and joy, they began to see rapid conversions. They were consumed, it seems, with a great burning desire to witness for Jesus.

According to Luke, Jesus described all this as a baptism in the Spirit (Acts 1:5), and it was with that baptism that the great apostolic prototype of revival began. The starting-point of all the extraordinary experiences that Acts describes and which constitute the fullness of the revival phenomenon, is to be found in that baptism which the early disciples received on the day of Pentecost. The great meetings in the Temple, the conviction of sin falling on the crowds and the great expansion of the Church were consequent upon that baptism. They would never have happened had not that initial group received a powerful outpouring of the Spirit. The number of that early band of disciples was absurdly small in relation to the impact that actually followed, but the baptism they received was abundantly sufficient to achieve God's purposes.

There has never been a revival since which has not had its beginnings in a similar impartation of this kind of baptism on some person or group of believers somewhere. Wherever we read of the Spirit of Conviction being powerfully at work or of mighty Gospel preaching being released, we invariably find that at the back of it there is some form of this baptism. So baptism in the Spirit and revival have never ceased to be inextricably bound together. At the heart of all revivals we find that a group or groups of believers have been mightily touched by the Spirit. As revival moves along, many others receive the same touch, and so the surge of impact continues. Such baptisms constitute one of the most important things we can pray for and look for.

In pursuing revival we need, therefore, to gain some understanding of the nature of this baptism in the Spirit. If we are pursuing revival blessing, and if baptism in the Spirit is foundational to revival, we need to know what it is and what it involves.

Jesus and the empowering of the Spirit

A good way of beginning our enquiry is to take full note of the fact that Jesus not only poured out the Spirit from a position of exaltation, but also Himself "received" the Spirit during His earthly life. This happened at the river Jordan at the beginning of His ministry and was witnessed by John the Baptist. John perceived a very clear connection between this coming of the Spirit on Jesus and Jesus' subsequent ministry of baptising with the Spirit. This is very apparent in his personal testimony, in which he said, "the one who sent me to baptise with water told me, 'the man on whom you see the Spirit come down and remain is he who will baptise with the Holy Spirit'" (John 1:33). Moreover, it is evident from the expression, "the one who sent me . . . told me" that the connection between the two was first planted in his mind by a revelation from God. This is a most significant connection, and it leads us to the obvious and natural inference that Jesus' ministry of baptising with the Spirit had something in common with His own receiving of the Spirit. So if we understand the one we will have some understanding of the other.

We have every right, therefore, to expect that a good deal of light should be thrown on the nature of the baptism of the Spirit by a careful examination of the coming of the Spirit on Jesus. In fact the more we study Luke's writings, the more evident this becomes. The two are very obviously linked in Luke's thought, and we can see real parallels between them as we put his Gospel and the Book of Acts side by side.

John the Baptist was very precise about what happened to Jesus when the Spirit came on Him. It was a very important moment for John, because it was a major sign by which he was to recognise the Messiah. He relates it as follows: "I saw the Spirit descend as a dove from heaven, and it remained on him" (John 1:32). If words mean anything at all, John is reporting that the Spirit actually came on Jesus. Nothing could be more clear than this. And nothing could be more theologically teasing than the implications of it, for John's words immediately challenge us with the fact that someone who already had the Spirit none the less received the Spirit. According to John, God simply told him that the Spirit would descend on Jesus and remain on Him. No attempt was made to reconcile this with the fact that Jesus had already been literally born of the Spirit and that, at the very least, he possessed the Spirit in all His wisdom. John's phraseology certainly does not betray any conflict in his own mind about this. His words are simple: "I saw the Spirit descend on him." They do not suggest that Jesus entered into an "appreciation" or "experience" or "realisation" of what was already present within Him as far as the Spirit was concerned. If we were to insist on understanding the event in that way, we should be in danger of violating plain language and breaking the first rule of biblical interpretation. We must allow this scripture to say what it means and mean what it says. The wording clearly says that the Spirit came on Jesus and then stayed on Him. The symbolic descent of the dove indicates the same thing. Jesus received the Spirit.

This episode indicates in principle, therefore, that though the Holy Spirit may have been present and even working at some depth within a person's life, it is still possible for that person, in another sense, to receive the Spirit. If this was true for Jesus Himself, then we have to accept that it could be true for us! Moreover, if we so wish, we can legitimately describe any such experience in terms of asking for and receiving the Spirit.

What was the significance and nature of this coming of the Spirit upon Jesus at the Jordan? This question was of immense interest to Luke, and in his gospel he pursued its meaning and implications carefully. We need to make plain the fact here that not only was Luke a very accurate historian, but he was also an able theologian. His historical narratives have a clear theological orientation, and it is not for us to dismiss this lightly but to seek to properly understand it. In other words, he did not simply describe experiences but sought to interpret them. This is certainly true in the case of the episode in which Jesus received the Spirit.

Luke found the key to understanding the nature of the Spirit's coming on Jesus in an explanation that Jesus Himself gave of it. He relates an occasion when Jesus took up a scroll in the synagogue at Nazareth and read from it the words of Isaiah 61:1-2, "the Spirit of the Lord is upon me, for he has anointed me to preach . . . to bind up . . . to proclaim liberty''. Jesus then sat down and claimed a personal fulfilment of that anointing. In his gospel Luke positions this episode in a sequence which clearly relates it to the happening at Jordan, and we are left in no doubt that, in Luke's view, Jesus perceived the receiving of the Spirit as being in the nature of an anointing for ministry.

We should notice the use of the word "anointing" here. It comes out of an Old Testament context, and there we find a consistent application of the term to ministry and service for the Lord. Anointing was appropriate for kings, priests and prophets (as well as others) and was symbolically representative of the pouring of the Spirit upon them to enable them to perform the function to which they were called.

It is perfectly obvious, not merely from Luke but also from the other gospels, that there was a new dimension in Jesus' life from the moment of His anointing. It was from that time that He began His ministry of preaching and healing and began to teach with authority. It was from that moment that the crowds began to follow Him and witness His working of extraordinary signs. The Holy Spirit had come upon Jesus at the Jordan, and there was now something additional in His life which had not been there before: the power (*dunamis*) of the Lord was now present with Him. He had entered into a new dimension of the Spirit which was to be of fundamental importance to Him in the work which His father expected Him to accomplish. He was anointed for ministry. Without it, despite all his understanding, He would have been unable to forward the work of the Kingdom.

The early church and the empowering of the Spirit

In his gospel, therefore, Luke obviously and accurately puts the coming of the Spirit on Jesus in the context of power for ministry. It seems perfectly clear that when he came to write his second volume (Acts), he put the coming of the

Spirit on the Church in precisely the same context. His theological perspective and interest had not changed. He did not, of course, associate the coming of the Spirit in the early Church with power for ministry purely in the interest of some theological theory. He did it for the simple reason that Jesus Himself had very clearly linked these two things. He had said, "you will receive power when the Holy Spirit comes on you; and you will be my witnesses" (Acts 1:8). The power (*dunamis*) of which Jesus was speaking was precisely the same as the power which He Himself had enjoyed after He had received the Spirit. Like the coming of the Spirit on Jesus, the coming of the Spirit on the disciples at Pentecost was to be an empowering.

It seems perfectly plain that it would never have occurred to Luke to consider the disciples as anything other than true believers before the Day of Pentecost. Jesus had taught them "by the Holy Spirit", and He was giving them commands He expected them to obey. They had in some sense already had the Spirit "breathed" on them (John 20:22–23).[1] The Holy Spirit had already been at work among them and they were believing witnesses to Jesus' death, resurrection and ascension. Martyn Lloyd-Jones rightly comments, "Now surely it is quite obvious that the apostles were regenerate and were children of God before the day of Pentecost."[2] Jesus commanded them to "wait in Jerusalem" not so that they could become believers but so that they could receive power to witness and fulfil God's purpose with a true dynamic. That, at any rate, is clearly Luke's perspective.

The words, "you will receive power when the Holy Spirit comes on you" are the only words spoken by Jesus in Acts which in any way directly explain and relate to the expression, "baptism in the Spirit". If we are to do justice to the term we must be prepared to accept this emphasis on empowering which, according to Luke, Jesus gave to it. This is all the more important because the term is very sparsely used in the New Testament. Apart from one exception, Luke is the only writer to use the term outside of the Gospels. Even in the Gospels the term is used only four times, and those four references (one in each Gospel) all refer to one event only, namely John's declaration that Jesus will baptise with the Spirit. We have already seen how closely that declaration is tied to Jesus' own receiving of the Spirit for service. There is therefore a consistency of context when we look at the expression, "baptise in the Spirit": it is used where power, ministry and service are the matters of concern. We need to be very careful indeed before we start applying it to explanations which are taken from other parts of the New Testament where the term is not in fact used.

In both his Gospel and Acts Luke displays an obvious interest in seeking to demonstrate the connection between the coming of the Spirit and powerful service in the Kingdom, and this interest is not difficult to understand. He was very much involved in ministry and mission and very much alive to the place of the Spirit in that work. Anything that helped him to understand the relation of the Spirit to ministry and mission was important to him. He was a convert of Paul's missions and an eyewitness to the power of the Holy Spirit which was so evident in those missions. He had, moreover, become an active co-worker with Paul. The whole subject of the Holy Spirit and His enabling power for ministry was, therefore, very close to his heart, and he could not pass over such critical moments as the anointing of Jesus with the Spirit and the coming of the Spirit on the Church for its witness without very thorough investigation. They were foundational to his understanding of his own experience, and they were crucial for the ongoing success of the Gentile mission.

In the light of this, the one thing that would be grossly unfair would be to fail to accord to Luke the theological competence to use his terms aright. He *is* theologically competent. His theological terminology, like his historical terminology, *is* accurate. It is based on careful notation of Jesus' own remarks. It is most important that we give full acceptance to the fact that in introducing the term "baptise in the Spirit" he is not writing from the perspective of the "sanctification" of believers, nor is he writing from the

135

perspective of "experiential assurance" in believers. It is very doubtful even that Luke is primarily concerned with any concept such as the "birth" of the Church. The growth, mission and ministry of the Church is his primary perspective, and for him "baptism in the Spirit" is the essential dynamic of that activity.

This is not to deny the fact that the "baptism in the Spirit" can have profound effects upon such areas as assurance and sanctification, as we shall see in the next chapter, nor is it to deny the fundamental importance of the work of the Spirit in regeneration. No real spiritual work of any kind can be done without the Holy Spirit. But to see the expression "baptism in the Spirit" as primarily descriptive of any of those aspects of spiritual experience is to associate with it areas of concern which the New Testament does not directly apply to it. It is noticeable, for example, that Paul does not import the expression into his discussion of sanctification and the Spirit in Romans 8. Undoubtedly, if we showed the same restraint and allowed it to remain in its proper biblical context we would avoid much confusion.[3]

"Baptism in the Spirit", therefore, has to do with empowering, with enabling, with equipment for ministry. As was the case in the ministry of Jesus, it is something different from the other operations of the Spirit and can follow after them. There is nothing really difficult in this: it really does make very good sense of the episodes in Acts in which people first believe and then receive the Spirit (in Luke's sense of receiving it for ministry). It is far more realistic than, for example, the extraordinary and tortuous attempts of some writers to make the believing Samaritans only sub-Christian until they received the Spirit.[4] And it makes very good sense of what happened on the Day of Pentecost. It allows us to accept simply and gladly the fact that for the one hundred and twenty, Pentecost was not a day of conversion but a day, as Jesus Himself said, of empowering.

Revival and the empowering of the Spirit

What has all this to do with revival? Simply this: in so far as Acts is a divine blueprint of all that makes up revival, it points to the fact that revival times will be times when people will experience something akin to a "baptism in the Spirit", when they will find the anointing of the Spirit coming upon them and empowering them for works of service and ministry. We may go further and say that before an awakening of unbelievers can take place the Spirit must fall upon those believers who are spiritually hungry with a dynamic sufficient to make them instruments of such an awakening. That is what happened on the Day of Pentecost, and that is what happened afterwards as others were added to the Church and received the same gift of the Spirit. It was in this way that Stephen and Philip were launched into their ministries, and it was in this way that other Christians, when scattered by persecution, gave such powerful and fruitful testimony to Christ. Revival means power, enabling, Spirit-filled ministry and witness flowing in wide streams out of the life of the Church.

I do not imagine for one moment that the few words of exposition concerning Acts 1 and 2 given above will be a convincing theological framework for all. But it must be true in general terms that the Spirit's presence in Acts has to be associated with great power in the Church. If there were a better theological framework which could lead us more clearly to recognise and appropriate that power, when such is clearly missing in the life of the Church, then I for one would gladly embrace it. It may well be the case that some hearts which are full of a great desire to see baptisms of power on the Church may express themselves in theological terms different to my own. I think I could live with that, provided there was a united desire of heart for that work of the Spirit which empowers the Church of Jesus, and a readiness to receive it in whatever form it might come.

The real fact of the matter is that there can be no doubt that again and again the first step to widespread awakenings and powerful movings of the Spirit amongst unbelievers has been a rediscovery of the enabling power of the Holy Spirit for the work of ministry. It has been a story of Christians who, though ministering faithfully for many a year, have been brought face to face with the need for a new dynamic in their lives. They have sought it and have been transformed. For some, such a "baptism" has come on them even without specific request, simply as an answer to deep inner longings. But always it has had to come. Empowering for the people of God for work that can in no way be done even by the regenerate heart alone is absolutely central to revival.

As an example of this, it is fascinating to see how God moved with His Spirit on those who were to be His instruments in the Welsh Revival of 1904. Jessie Penn Lewis, giving a sort of district-by-district survey of this activity of the Spirit, wrote:

In the Bridgend district we find the Spirit of God at work many months before the spiritual high-tide came upon the land. Several of the ministers received the power of the Holy Ghost in August, 1903. One was the Pastor of a prominent church, the worldly reputation of which was an almost insuperable obstacle to aggressive Christian work. When he entered the Spirit-filled life his church immediately felt the change.

She records that

in the Neath district we find the Holy Spirit moving in a large mission hall holding two thousand people. The pastor received the "anointing" some thirteen years ago, and hence was ready for the tide when it came.

Speaking of the Monmouthshire district, she notes:

the Pastor of one church writes that after his return from the 1904 Llandrindod Conference, not a prayer meeting, church meeting, or any other service took place without the message concerning the whole-hearted reception of the Spirit being urged upon his people, until in October two ministers in the experience of the Spirit-filled life came to conduct special services, when the whole church was transformed, the entire diaconate received blessing.[5]

Jessie Penn Lewis goes on to cite other examples of this activity of the Spirit, and they are valuable simply because they reveal the widespread nature of that activity and show that it was not just amongst the well-known leaders of the revival that it took place.

Of course, there is no question at all of the fact that when we look at the noted leaders of the revival, such as Evan Roberts, R. B. Jones, W. W. Lewis and Keri Evans, we find the Spirit moving in fresh power on them. They all experienced the Spirit of God coming on them and transforming their ministries. Keri Evans, for example, wrote:

I was baptised with floods of living, mighty transforming power for about half an hour. The experience was so marvellously invigorating and renewing that I sought it again the next day with the same result.[6]

R. B. Jones, in a memorable interview with F. B. Meyer, told him that he wanted the Holy Spirit. Meyer said to Jones, "You want the Spirit? Well, take hold of Him, then." He did precisely that. Describing this experience later, he wrote: "A new world opened up to me . . . Next Sunday I said nothing, but they [his congregation] knew a new man was in the pulpit."[7] A new world opened up also for the many who heard his preaching in the months of revival that followed:

Evan Roberts prayed for the Spirit for thirteen years, saying to himself, "I will have the Spirit." Finally, during a mission led by Seth Joshua he was pressed to cry out, "Bend me, O Lord!" He later described what followed in these words:

139

I felt a living force coming into my bosom. This grew and grew, and I was almost bursting . . . After I was bent a wave of peace came over me . . . Henceforth the salvation of souls became the burden of my heart.[8]

It was a bending and a baptism that set Wales alight.

It is the same story whenever and wherever we see God powerfully at work in the world and preparing people for revival. In 1953 revival began to spread over what was then the Belgian Congo (now Zaire), bringing a "tornado of blessing". A lady missionary wrote of her own preparation of heart prior to the coming of that blessing:

One night, burdened for souls and praying for enduement from on high, and whilst rededicating myself to His service, a strange sensation came over me, my heart was pounding, prayer was pouring out of me, and my body began to tremble. I was afraid, for I felt that I was probably allowing my emotions to overcome me, and I tried to still this strange experience. From that day I found the messages to the girls charged with new power, power from on high.[9]

She goes on to say that she came to accept the somewhat frightening experience. It was repeated during a further time of prayer:

Now recognising it for what it was I did not resist: it seemed that another being had taken possession of me, as indeed was true; the Holy Ghost had come, surging through my body and reaching even to my finger tips . . . My heart and my whole being were praising God.

She had become a prepared instrument of spiritual awakening.

These accounts are numberless. Marie Monsen in China had an extraordinary vision of the glory of God flowing down over a kneeling figure and then on into a desert. She knew that the figure was herself, and that the glory of God was the Spirit flowing. She realised that there was an experience of the Spirit to be had, so she sought God until she received it. Then indeed she found that the river flowed on through her into the spiritual wastes of China.[10] James Fraser came out of Lisuland, where he had seen powerful revivings, speaking of the Holy Spirit as "a blessing we should claim".[11] Charles Finney, witness of so much revival activity, said:

> I was converted on the morning of Oct. 10th. In the evening of the same day and on the following morning I received overwhelming baptisms of the Holy Ghost. I found myself endued with such power from on high that a few words dropped here and there to individuals were the means of their immediate conversion.[12]

D. L. Moody received the Spirit on the streets of New York in 1871 and as a result became an infinitely more powerful flame for God than he had ever been before, bringing thousands into the Kingdom on both sides of the Atlantic. Andrew Murray, Samuel Chadwick, R. A. Torrey, William Booth, Rees Howells and a whole host of other powerful men and women of God had no hesitation in speaking of the experience of power which God put upon them through the Spirit.

The Pentecostal witness and modern experience

Such testimony was very clear, therefore, even before the outbreak of that particular witness to the baptism in the Spirit which took place at the turn of the century and which led to the emergence of the Pentecostal churches. In the Pentecostal witness there was, of course, a very clear emphasis on the fact that baptism in the Spirit was linked to ministry and service for God. The distinctive feature of this Pentecostal witness was that it brought into prominence the fact that all the gifts of the Spirit which had a bearing on ministry were to be expected in the Church and were to be fully embraced. The ministry of healing and deliverance was to be fully accepted and restored to its proper place. Words of knowledge and wisdom were to find their place once more, as was the gift of prophecy. The gift of tongues was, of course, very much to be included, and all this was to be expected alongside the unction to preach and witness. This was the new dimension of the baptism in the Spirit which the spiritual explosion at Azusa Street in 1904 released.

The subsequent decades of this century have abundantly confirmed the essential truth of this Pentecostal witness. The presence of such baptisms in the Spirit, with the free flowing of spiritual gifts, has been a mark of some of the greatest revival movements of the century. We have now reached a point where the Pentecostal churches have become the single largest evangelical grouping in the world-wide Christian Church. That in itself vindicates a claim to "power for witness". In less than ninety years it has outstripped the other groupings, most of which have for most of those years rejected the Pentecostal witness. The truth of this testimony is secure, therefore, despite undoubted excesses and aberrations at times.

Perhaps one of the greatest contributions of the Pentecostal witness has been the consistent challenge to lay hold of an enduement with power which it has brought to all its followers. It may well be that this is what has led to constant and, in some cases, amazing growth. Previously this widespread challenge that all should be empowered had not always been quite so clearly brought before the Church. The Welsh revival of 1904, for example, saw thousands of people accepting the Word of God and coming into living faith, but how much was accomplished in terms of bringing such converts into an enduement of power is another matter. As we shall see later, two of its greatest converts, the Jeffreys brothers, had no such enduement until they found it through the Pentecostal witness. It is true that there had been men in an earlier generation, like C. T. Studd, who had invariably and immediately led their converts to "ask for the Spirit", and there were writers like Andrew Murray, R. A. Torrey and Samuel Chadwick who urged upon their readers the need to seek the power of the Spirit, but in the general life of the evangelical churches this vital emphasis seemed to be lacking.

The last three decades have seen the Pentecostal witness broaden its impact through the emergence of the charismatic renewal. In its initial stages in the sixties this began with people in the mainline denominations receiving remarkable experiences of the baptism in the Spirit. Many leaders quickly followed the Pentecostals in calling for people to look for such a baptism. The result was widespread and powerful experiences of the presence of the Holy Spirit. The testimony that had been kept at bay for so many years was at last finding its way into the wider context in which God had undoubtedly wanted it to be from the first − namely, the whole of the Church.

There has been a tendency, however, especially among leading charismatic Anglicans, to associate baptism in the Spirit with the conversion experience, so making one full initiation experience. This appears to have its root more than anything in a desire to build bridges with evangelicals who still find such a Pentecostal testimony difficult. Whether they are right or not remains to be seen. The real issue at stake, however, is whether such an all-embracing idea of initiation will actually promote a real searching after enduement for power, or whether it will obscure a vision of the need of such enduement by leaving people to think that because they are converted they must needs have all God wants them to have. One wonders whether such a view will provide a proper basis for the sort of ministry which will help those who are converted and yet are hungry for further blessing to find the answer to their desire. If it does, as those who hold it claim it does, then it will be a friend of revival. If not, it will hinder. The important thing is that the Church becomes full of people who are themselves full of the Spirit and moving in His anointings. Theology and practice will ultimately be tested by whether or not they permit and facilitate that.

We need hardly say that this Pentecostal/charismatic witness is very akin to the pattern in Acts. Enduement with power and the phenomenon of spiritual gifts are written on every page of Luke's account of the life of the early Church. No one has ever denied that the early Church had such power, not even those who have most bitterly opposed the idea that this power has at times reappeared during the subsequent history of the Church. Our present century has taught us by demonstrable fact and powerful growth in the world-wide Church that the re-establishment of a full experience of baptism in the Spirit, with all accompanying gifts, has been God's purpose.

* * *

It is time to draw the threads together. Revivals have always followed the pattern of Acts, and Acts points unmistakably to the Church being baptised with power as an essential groundwork for all else that happens in terms of spiritual awakening in the world. It is inconceivable that the three thousand would have been convicted of their sin and saved without there being such a prepared instrument as Peter. There would have been no great teaching and prayer gatherings in the Temple without there being a team of apostles endued with power to preach and to teach.

There have always been enduements with power on people whenever there have been revivals. Such enduements, such baptisms of the Spirit, are an integral and fundamental basis for revivals. Wesley wrote of himself and Whitefield that "the power of God came mightily upon us"; Howell Harris frequently referred to the extraordinary visitation by the Spirit which he once experienced in the quietness of a church tower. Whatever the particulars of each case, the same pattern is always evident. Revivals require men and women of God who are endued with power for ministry. If men and women are to preach to the crowds as Jesus preached to them, they need to follow the Master in His receiving of the anointing of the Spirit.

In the light of this, we should not be surprised that after so much prayer for revival in the 1950s God should have answered by a movement in which a very large number of people came into the blessing which is most commonly referred to as baptism in the Spirit. It may well only be a first stage or a basis of what we commonly call revival, but there can be no doubt at all that it is part and parcel of the process by which God brings in full revival blessing. It is at least possible that what has happened in the widespread experience of the baptism in the Spirit will prove to be a very necessary preparation for a full revival outpouring. That, at any rate, was the feeling expressed by some in the early days of the charismatic movement, and it is still the opinion of many after nearly three decades.[13] The renewal has not yet seen the awe, majesty and holiness associated with widespread awakenings, and it has not yet manifested the burning spirit of witness that has been such a feature of them, but this does not mean that these things will not in due course follow. Indeed, if we are prepared to go beyond what has already been given and earnestly to implore God to complete what He has so obviously begun, then we shall not be disappointed. The failure will come if, when we have experienced an enduement which has been thrilling and even transforming, we do not go on to seek God for everything else that can flow with that enduement. We need to press on from renewal to all that God can do in revival.

Notes

1. The attempt to harmonise John's account of the receiving of the Spirit with that of Acts is not an easy exercise. If one were to attempt such a reconciliation it would need to be in terms of relating each account to its context and noting the specific reason for which the Spirit was given in each case. We have no other clear guidelines. A different purpose for

the coming of the Spirit is indicated in each. In John the purpose expressed is to declare forgiveness of sins. The prime purpose of the Spirit's coming at Pentecost is to enable for witness.

2. In his book *Joy Unspeakable* Martyn Lloyd-Jones constantly takes this position.

3. It is interesting that in a book like *Joy Unspeakable*, where various aspects of the baptism in the Spirit are considered, Lloyd-Jones should affirm (p. 137), "Baptism with the Holy Spirit is primarily and essentially a baptism with power."

4. E.g. James Dunn, *Baptism in the Spirit*. Equally tortuous, in my opinion, are the attempts to make the experience of the Samaritans something abnormal, e.g. Michael Green, *I believe in the Spirit*, p. 167.

5. Jessie Penn-Lewis, *The Awakening in Wales*, p. 25ff.

6. B. P. Jones, *The King's Champions*, p. 41.

7. Ibid., p. 49.

8. Oswald J. Smith, *The Revival We Need*, p. 42. This is one of a series of graphic descriptions of such enduements.

9. *This is That* (CLC), p. 23.

10. Marie Monsen, *The Awakening*, p. 115. In the same book she tells the remarkable story of the intense battle which she fought to secure the anointing of which the vision spoke. Such baptisms are bitterly contested.

11. J. O. Fraser, *Behind the Ranges* p. 243 (republished as *Mountain Rain*).

12. Oswald J. Smith, op. cit., p. 38.

13. Peter Hocken, *Streams of Renewal*, p. 173.

We have too largely forgotten the exhortation: "Be filled with the Spirit." We have thought that the fullness of the Spirit was a speciality for the apostolic age, instead of being for all time. And thus the majority of Christians are living on the other side of Pentecost. We can never be what we might be until we have got back to apostolic theory and practice in respect of this essential matter. Oh that God, in these last days, would raise up some fire-touched tongue to do for this neglected doctrine what Luther did for justification by faith!

F. B. Meyer

Chapter 9: Baptised in the Spirit (2)

I saw the Spirit come down from heaven as a dove and remain on him.

John 1:32

They saw what seemed to be tongues of fire that separated and came to rest on each one of them.

Acts 2:3

A deeper side to baptism in the Spirit

In the last chapter we saw that baptisms in the Spirit are an essential part of the scene of revival. We have talked of such baptisms in terms of enduement of power and anointing. They are to be prayed for and expected. It is my concern in this chapter to draw attention to the fact that these baptisms frequently involve a feature which could be considered as being deeper even than the release of "gifts" or the release of liberty and boldness in speaking. This deeper factor can be described as a revelation of God or a powerful experience of some aspect of the character and nature of God (Father, Son or Spirit).

It is the process by which the outpouring of the Spirit brings a new and vivid insight into some feature of God's nature and then makes people, in Peter's words, "partakers of that divine nature" (2 Peter 1:4). In other words we are talking about an experience in which we see something of the nature of God at a level so deep that we ourselves are made to feel as though that nature is invading our own lives and becoming part of us. It is what happened to Isaiah when he first had a revelation of the holiness of God. He felt the purging of that holiness entering his own being (Isaiah 6:1ff).

This element of revelation is something which has always been present in the most powerful baptisms in the Spirit. It has been a crucially important source of motivation for God's people in the work of the Kingdom. It is revelation of a kind that has instigated and sustained dynamic calls to service for God. Not only that, but such revelation, burning in the hearts of those who have received it, has become the foundation for the most potent preaching and teaching of the Word, particularly in times of revival. Consequently, when we are praying for anointings and baptisms it is most important that we have this matter of revelation in our hearts. We must thoroughly understand such experiences and urge the need of it before the Lord.

Baptisms of love

We can begin to understand such revelations of God as a part of baptism in the Spirit by once more going to the account of the anointing of Jesus. When we examine the four accounts of it in the gospels we find that each one tells us that the Spirit came on Jesus "as a dove". Whether it was the literal alighting of a dove or whether it was a visionary experience, we cannot say. But whatever it was, it was clearly a sign from God indicating the nature of the anointing. Such signs are never without point or purpose. What, then, was the connection between a dove and an anointing for ministry? A dove hardly conveys the impression of power, and yet it was the symbol of the anointing that rested on Jesus.

The symbolic possibilities of the dove are many, but two at least must stand out: peace and love. Jesus was being anointed for ministry, and the dove indicated that the inherent nature of that ministry was to be one of gentleness, peace, compassion and love. This was indeed precisely how Jesus ministered. When the disciples wanted to call down fire upon the Samaritans He had remind them that they belonged to a different Spirit — a Spirit of peace (Luke 9:55). He was moved with compassion by the tired and hungry crowds, and by a bereaved mother (Luke 7:13). Again and again love motivated Him to minister. His gentle, peaceable spirit wept over the prospect of the judgement that was to come upon Jerusalem. He loved his disciples and it was a love of patience, friendship and total commitment.

We can see, therefore, the very beautiful and very powerful motivating force of love and compassion running right through Jesus' ministry. The power of this force was perhaps best expressed by John when he wrote. "God so loved . . . that He gave His only Son . . . " It was out of love that Jesus came to save us, and likewise it was out of love that He exercised His earthly ministry. There is certainly ample evidence in human life and behaviour of the immense release of courage, power and sustained action which can spring from a heart of love.

We need to be quite clear in our minds, however, that the coming of the dove on Jesus was not merely a sign of the kind of attitude which His Father expected Him to adopt in His ministry. It was not a sort of visual reminder to Him that He had come as an ambassador of peace. It was something very much more than that. It was nothing less than the Holy Spirit settling on Him personally with all His love, gentleness, peace and compassion. All the graces of the nature of the Spirit which the dove symbolises came on Jesus. Here was an anointing indeed − an anointing of love. It was a real partaking of the Spirit's love. That is why Jesus' ministry was so peaceable, so gentle. That is why He did not quench the smoking flax! He flowed with the Spirit of gentleness. Powerful though His preaching was and amazing as His healings were, they were all accomplished in the flow of the Spirit of compassion − the same Spirit who gave Him words of knowledge and wisdom gave Him also great love. As the Spirit came to rest upon Jesus in this dove-like manner, therefore He must have sensed afresh and at great depth the love and compassion of the Father for the people to whom He was being sent. Out of that revelation flowed the motivation for His ministry and the courage He needed to face the Cross.

It is not difficult to find a similar revelation of the love of God amongst those who, like Jesus, have received an anointing for service. If we go back to the nineteenth century and to such a great figure in revival as Finney, we find that his baptism in the Spirit not only released immediate power into his preaching but also filled him with love. In describing his baptism Finney has this to say:

> the Holy Spirit descended upon me in a manner that seemed to go through me, body and soul. I could feel the impression, like a wave of electricity, going through and through. Indeed it seemed to come in waves of liquid love; for I could not express it in any other way . . . No words can express the wonderful love that was shed abroad in my heart . . . I fell asleep, but almost as soon awoke again on account of the great flow of the love of God that was in my heart. I was so filled with love that I could not sleep.[1]

Howell Harris was an extraordinary instrument in the revivals that flowed over Wales in the middle decades of the eighteenth century. He was a great friend of the Wesleys and Whitefield and was powerful in exhorting and organising. Three weeks after his conversion, whilst seeking God in a village church, he received a baptism of power. Martyn Lloyd-Jones calls it the "crucial experience which turned him into a flaming evangelist".[2] Harris describes the experience thus:

> Suddenly I felt my heart melting within me like wax before a fire, and love to God for my Saviour. I felt not only love and peace, but a longing to die and to be with Christ. Then there came a cry into my soul that I have never known before — "Abba, Father!"

Later he described this as the day in which the love of God was shed abroad in his heart. Lloyd-Jones comments "This is what created within him a passion for the lost. This is what urged him to go out and to tell the people about their condition and do something about them." Harris himself wrote: "Were it not for the love I tasted, I should have given up; I never could have gone against the current. Love fell in showers on my soul, so that I could scarcely contain myself."[3] D. L. Moody says of his baptism in the Spirit in New York: "I can only say that God revealed Himself to me, and I had such an experience of His love that I had to ask Him to stay His hand. I went to preaching again. The sermons were not different; I did not present any new truths and yet hundreds were converted."[4]

Evan Roberts cried out to God to bend him. Saying "What bent me was God commending his love, and I not seeing anything in it to commend." As he allowed himself to be bent, "the Holy Ghost came and melted his whole being by a revelation of the love of God at Calvary".[5]

The inner transformation and the motivating power of these experiences of the love of God are obvious in these lives. It is not only that ministry gifts became evident, but the love of God brought a beautifully fragrant and exceedingly powerful dynamic. The apostle Paul had the same kind of experience, declaring that "Christ's love constrains us" (2 Corinthians 5:14) and that "God has poured out his love into our hearts by the Holy Spirit" (Romans 5:5). Perhaps one of the tragedies of our more modern approach to the baptism of the Spirit is that we are often more concerned with the gifts associated with it than with the revelation of God's love that has been at other times so much a part of it. Of course, it is never really an "either-or" matter. We need both the gifts and the revelation of love. But so frequently we seem to be unable to hold both together, and at our worst moments we even pit one against the other through sheer fleshly enthusiasm or doctrinal pride! If a baptism is to be of the most powerful kind it will certainly involve both these aspects.

Baptisms of fiery tongues

As the Spirit came on the disciples on the Day of Pentecost they too were allowed the privilege of a symbolic vision along with their baptism. It was not, however, a vision of a dove. Instead "they saw what seemed to be tongues of fire that separated and came to rest on each one of them". This vision was not ushered in by anything so quiet as the gentle descent of the dove, but by a sudden sound like the "blowing of a violent wind". This is a very different and contrasting symbolism, and it is interesting to discern what it meant.

In order to do that, the first thing we need to note is that what rested over their heads was a tongue. It is fairly obvious what a tongue is intended to represent: speech and talking! It is reasonably easy to accept the idea of the Spirit being symbolised as a dove − it points to His love and His peace. But the Spirit as a tongue? There is no real difficulty here, of course, once we recognise that the Holy Spirit is a witness and therefore speaks (Acts 5:32). He is a Spirit who bears witness to Jesus − that was the burden of Jesus' teaching about the Spirit at the Last Supper. He had warned His disciples on one occasion that when they were brought before rulers they were not to wonder what they should say, for the Spirit would give them the necessary words. At Pentecost the Spirit as the great Spokesman of God came powerfully upon them. It was the great need of the hour. The work of Jesus had been accomplished and now people had to know about it. The Church had to be built: people had to hear and believe. The Spirit wanted the hearts of God's people, but He also wanted their tongues, for witness had to be given.

We must bear in mind here that the Holy Spirit as a witness does not move simply out of a sense of duty! The Spirit moves with an intense desire and eagerness to speak out. It is the chief delight of the Spirit to witness to Jesus and all that Jesus has accomplished. There is the same compulsion with the Spirit to witness to Jesus as there was first with the Father to send Jesus, and then with Jesus to fulfil His Father's will. It is a compulsion of love and desire. At Pentecost the Spirit was among the disciples with an overwhelming desire to speak out for Jesus and bring His Church into being.

This intense eagerness of the Spirit gives us some indication of why the vision given to the disciples was not simply a tongue, but a "tongue of fire". When a tongue is on fire, it is a sign of the fervour and conviction with which a person speaks. Moreover, the tongue that is on fire always burns into the hearts of those who hear. When a person witnesses out of burning conviction, those who are listening will come under a similar conviction. This is how spiritual fire burns and is transmitted.

This, then, is what is signified by the fact that the tongues that rested on the disciples were tongues of fire. Moreover, in the same way that the dove was not a mere reminder to Jesus of the love of God but was something much more, so the disciples were not just being reminded of the duty to witness but were being given the fire of the Spirit to do it. They were not being exhorted to greater effort. They were actually drinking-in of that heart-burning desire to witness which belongs to the Spirit. What was being revealed to them was the greatness of the Father's desire to communicate all the work that had been done through His Son. From that moment there was within them a divine fire, a divine compulsion to speak out.

It was a baptism in the Spirit of a kind that the Church desperately needs again. It is this sort of baptism that makes evangelism the force it needs to be. It is this sort of baptism that we urgently need to seek for the Church.

All that was happening to those early disciples was borne out in the most remarkable way by the fact that, as the symbolic vision of tongues of fire rested on them, they all began to speak out "as the Spirit gave them utterance". The Spirit wanted to speak, and here they were speaking! Even more remarkable was the fact that they spoke in languages they had never learned. What a glorious confirmation that the Spirit of utterance and witness rested upon them! The

155

words they were speaking were not their words — they had never learned them and could not understand them — they were the words of the Spirit. Here was the Spirit giving expression to the great longing in the divine heart that witness should be made throughout the earth in all its languages. Here was the Spirit declaring the great things God had done.

The early Church was blessed, therefore, with a great dynamic of desire and compulsion to witness. The eagerness was burning in them: it was heart-witness, not head-witness. Moreover, it was bold witness. The Spirit who bears witness is afraid of no one, whether they be threatening rulers or scoffers. He has them in derision! This divine boldness was clearly a hallmark of those early Christians. It rested on the apostles as they bore witness to the crowds in the Temple and to the rulers in the Sanhedrin, and it later came on Stephen and Philip as they, in their turn, faced the same rulers. When persecution arose "those who were scattered" none the less went about preaching the Word. Whether they were scattered to Samaria, Cyprus or Antioch, it was always the same story: they bore witness, and they also bore fruit. There were moments, of course, when they felt shock waves of fear, particularly when they saw the apostles thrown into prison and heard the threats of the authorities. There was immediate recourse, however, to prayer for a fresh infilling of the divine boldness — and they were not disappointed.

This eager, compelling, witnessing Spirit coming to rest upon believers is a most powerful expression of the baptism in the Spirit. It is this that produces that sense of great unrest in the heart of the missionary. He sees some untouched tribe and cannot rest until some contact has been made, some communication of the Gospel has been given. It impels a Hudson Taylor to inland China, a Henry Martyn to Arabia. It produces the kind of effect which Jeremiah experienced when he described the Word of the Lord as a burning in his inward parts. Even though he determined to say nothing, the Spirit of God wrestled until he was compelled to speak. It produces that inward prompting among the ranks of those great personal soul-winners which makes them approach and speak to particular people in the most unlikely situations, and with great effect. It leads a George Dempster to witness to tramps, many of whom thereupon find their way back to God and to society. It manifests itself in that extraordinary experience of exhilaration and deep satisfaction which comes during times of preaching in the open air or witnessing on the streets, an exhilaration and satisfaction which is not human but reveals the heart of the Spirit Himself.

Baptisms of holiness

The Spirit came "in bodily form like a dove" and the Spirit came like "tongues of fire that separated and rested on each of them." Both of those comings indicate a particular emphasis or dynamic, and both issue in ministry and service. There is, however, nothing to suggest that there may not be other emphases, other revelations, given by the Spirit as he comes in power upon the people of God. Indeed, the very fact that Luke presents us with two such contrasting experiences of the coming of the Spirit should make us very ready to be open to other manifestations, equally dynamic and motivating.

For instance, there is no doubt that the Spirit has come upon people with a powerful manifestation of God's holiness. We could refer once again to Isaiah and the extraordinary vision he received of God in all His holiness. Isaiah was broken by the vision, recognised his own uncleanness and then felt the purging coal touch his lips. This experience did not stop at his own personal cleansing, but concluded with the call issued by the Lord, "Who will go for us?" Isaiah responded immediately with, "Here I am. Send me." Thus began an empowered and anointed prophetic ministry to a sinful and backsliding Judah. God knew the ministry He wanted and accordingly He burned into the heart of His servant the nature of His holiness. From that moment Isaiah was certainly an anointed spokesman in God's hands. Such visions are of course revelations given by the Spirit, and clearly they constitute not merely a call but an empowering for ministry.

In the previous chapter we mentioned how God dealt with many pastors and leaders prior to the Welsh revival of 1904 and endued them with power for service. We need to add here that the experiences of these men undoubtedly carried with them a very deep impress and revelation of the holiness of God. The anointings which came to one after another of these men had this emphasis. For example, R. B. Jones, one of the foremost preachers in the revival, wrote of a pastor who was "well read, cultured, possessed of a mind penetrating and analytical to a degree" but for whom eternal realities were just "so many postulates of thought and nothing more". Jones described what happened to this man as the Spirit came on him:

A day came when the reality of God as a Person and a Holy Presence seemed to dawn on his soul. The consequence was that . . . his church soon realised that it had a pastor of an unusual, and altogether new type. The preaching, while it had lost nothing of its brilliant intellectuality, was concerned with a new message and charged with a power that was overwhelming. The holiness of the Lord had become to him a thing of tremendous reality; he himself had stood in its humbling light, and now his people also were searched by the same pitilessly searching and inescapable rays.[6]

This pastor was in fact W. S. Jones, another great leader of the revival. He gave his own account of this "visitation":

Suddenly there came to me an indelible consciousness of the amazing holiness of God. Like a purifying fire — like a fiery river flowing out from the throne — and I in the midst as if reclining on it. I do not know whether I were in the body or out of it but the fire percolated through my whole nature. I remember the thought gripped me —

"the Holiness of God, and I am still alive in the midst of the stream. I cannot die here."[7]

Another writer comments:

> After his strange experience of baptism with fire, W. S. Jones began to preach with devastating power the need for every man to yield utterly to Christ's Lordship as the only gateway to the real life of holiness.

This extraordinary experience of the holiness of God was the predominant characteristic of the Welsh Revival preachers. It was something that God seemed to lay on all of them. R. B. Jones himself was, in the words of his own people at Salem, a "John the Baptist". Holiness burned throughout his messages.

Perhaps one of the most tantalising stories in Scripture is in fact that of John the Baptist himself. Relatively little is said in the Bible about the enormous depths of his spiritual experience, and the treasure of that experience lies mostly hidden. We do know, however, that he was "filled with the Spirit" from his mother's womb, which, in Luke's theological terminology, means that the anointing rested on him from the moment of his birth. We also know that he came to Israel with a devastating message of holiness and repentance from sin. There seems little doubt that the anointing from birth brought great consciousness to his own soul of the need for simple, holy living and strict personal discipline. That much is obvious from the style of his early life. All through his life there was burned into him the truth of the holiness of God. When the right moment came, his revelation of that holiness broke over a whole country with enormous effect.

All this, incidentally, should make us rather more aware of why it was that over considerable periods, and especially in the latter part of the nineteenth century, baptism with the Spirit was so closely connected with holiness. Experiences and revelations of the holiness of God, which in their way were akin to that of Isaiah, were profoundly real to very many people and thoroughly purged out a gross tendency to sin. Such people came out of those experiences with a deep sense of having been made holy. They discovered that when some aspect of God is made abundantly clear to the heart by the Spirit, that heart actually becomes a partaker of what is revealed. After such a baptism of holiness their sense of victory over sin and their desire no longer to remain in sin were immensely enhanced. Though they sometimes fell into sin again, they knew that in a very real way they had been sanctified. Theologically the case might, in the opinion of others, have been overstated, but we should not despise their testimony on account of our own particular formulations of the process of sanctification. Would to God the baptisms of our own generation saw more revelations of the holiness of God and moments of crisis resulting in such purification!

Double blessing!

We have distinguished the different emphases which have characterised moments of baptism in the Spirit simply to show that it can come to people in a number of different ways. There is no good reason why a number of these characteristics should not be simultaneously revealed in a baptism in the spirit. In fact this seems normally to be the case. For example, Brengle, the much loved Salvationist, had a remarkable experience of love and holiness flowing together. He described it as follows:

> While [I was] reading some of the words of Jesus, He gave me such a blessing as I never dreamed a man could have this side of heaven. It was an unutterable revelation. It was a heaven of love that came into my heart. My soul melted like wax before fire. I sobbed and sobbed. I loathed myself that I had ever sinned against Him or doubted Him or lived for myself and not for His glory. Every ambition for self was now gone. The pure flame of love burned it like a blazing fire would burn a moth.[8]

Here was love and holiness intermingled: it was a revelation of love burning up self. Brengle was by no means alone in this. This has been a familiar theme and experience among very many people. It was very characteristic of John Wesley. Love and holiness were the great motivators of his life. Perhaps we need to stand back and discover once again the intimate relationship that exists between the love of God and holiness of God.

If we were to examine the experience of the disciples on the Day of Pentecost we might well find that though the predominant impress was of the witnessing Spirit, there was also a manifestation of the love of the Spirit. It is difficult to imagine them having a longing to witness that was not associated with the love of God. Moreover, it is quite clear from the way in which those early disciples loved each other and took care of each other that their hearts had been filled with a great love by the Spirit.

Recognising and seeking such baptisms

Baptism in the Spirit is not, therefore, an enduement of power which is simply a matter of gifts of ministry, powerful and necessary as those gifts are. Baptism in the Spirit is also the provision of personal spiritual revelation and understanding which powerfully enervates and undergirds ministry. Peter Hocken, investigating the early years of the charismatic movement, makes this point very firmly, commenting that the definition "of baptism in the Spirit in terms of empowerment for ministry does not in fact do justice to the event of baptism in the Spirit as it is described in countless testimonies. In particular, it makes no reference to the element that is so central in many testimonies, namely a new level of knowledge of Jesus Christ, and some awareness of the love of the Father and the distinctiveness of the Holy Spirit."[9] It is difficult to disagree with this view. Many who have experienced a baptism in the Spirit have testified to remarkable new dimensions of biblical understanding, to an appreciation of the Holy Spirit as a teacher, to new revelation of the importance of prayer and fasting, to a much clearer recognition of spiritual conflict with powers of darkness which they had only dimly perceived before. The range of impact is very wide.

We should be very careful, however, that while recognising this powerful dimension of revelation, we do not fail to give the baptism of the Spirit its fundamental context of an empowering. Of course such revelations will give immense personal blessing and will bring assurances to us which we never had before. Of course they will be very much in the nature of a seal. But that is not God's prime intention in giving them. His concern is His greater glory. His concern is the work that can be done through us. All those who have been His instruments for accomplishing His purposes have first had to have powerful revelations of His person which have given their ministry a sharp cutting edge. It is impossible otherwise. The greatest ministries have always gone alongside the greatest revelations. The testimony of Scripture and of so many saints is that God comes upon His people with His revelations and His anointings because He has ministry for them to do.

Such baptisms are not an initiatory experience, if by that we mean an initiation into Christ and into his salvation. They are not to be confused with the new birth. The coming of the Spirit upon Jesus can only be described as initiatory in the sense of initiation into ministry. There is no indication that the coming of the Spirit at Pentecost was initiatory. The apostles had already had the Spirit breathed on them, they were committed to Jesus and approved by Him, and apparently they had already been baptised before the Day of Pentecost. As Peter Hocken has said, the charismatic testimony has been one of a "new level of knowledge" of Jesus Christ, not one of a beginning of such knowledge. That testimony, like that of the Pentecostal churches, is to deeper revelations, deeper understandings, deeper experiences. Baptism in the Spirit as something beyond initial Christian experience was, of course, a fact well recognised before the advent of the charismatic witness.

Such a view was by no means solely advocated by Pentecostals, and was voiced in some quarters before they appeared on the scene. In the minds of those who actually experienced such blessing, baptism in the Spirit was constantly and predominantly linked with power for and release into ministry.

It is very important that this context is maintained. Once the prevailing viewpoint is one which merges the experience of enduement with power into normal Christian beginnings we are in great danger of losing the experience. Only if our concept of normal Christian beginnings is radically altered, and we consistently include within it a call to baptism in the Spirit as well as to regeneration, will this all-important dimension of Christian experience be preserved.

If it ceases to be preached, it will cease to be sought after. If it ceases to be taught, then, those who seek after deeper blessing and feel the need of something more in the way of dynamic for their Christian work will be in danger of going away unsatisfied.

* * *

Revival, then, is a time of great release of such baptisms in the Spirit. It is a time when Jesus pours out His Spirit, when those who already have the Spirit may yet receive a new experience of Him. The sparking-point for everything else that takes place in revival is to be found in such baptisms. That, at any rate, is the simple testimony of history. These baptisms alone have produced the spiritual thrust that has made the Church glorious before God and the world. The revelation of the glory of God is a particularly beautiful part of such baptisms, a part we need to keep very much more in mind than we do at present.

If we are going to see preaching which has a fire and a depth within it and which can powerfully impact the world, then it must be preaching which has such baptisms and such revelations as its foundation. Orthodoxy alone will never do. True spiritual work at the deepest level of

163

the human heart is what is required. For that we must seek after God.

We should pray for such baptisms, therefore. We should preach for them and above all receive them as they are granted to us. We should be ready to acknowledge that when they come they may well come with all the power with which they came at Pentecost. We must accept that unless such baptisms do come, we shall not see stamped upon our generation the message that God so longs to hear and see proclaimed.

Notes

1. Quoted by R. Edman, *They Found the Secret*, p. 55. Edman's book is a brief but fascinating survey of the deeper workings of the Spirit in the lives of a number of people who have been much used of God in His service.
2. Martyn Lloyd-Jones, *The Puritan*, p. 282. This quotation is from a full chapter about Harris.
3. Richard Bennett, *Howell Harris and the Dawn of Revival*, p. 30.
4. R. Edman, op. cit., p. 84.
5. Jessie Penn Lewis, *The Awakening in Wales*, p. 18.
6. R. B. Jones, *Rent Heavens*, p. 28.
7. B. P. Jones, *The King's Champions*, p. 37.
8. R. Edman, op. cit., p. 26.
9. Peter Hocken, *Streams of Renewal*, p. 169.

Chapter 10: Conviction of Sin

When he comes, he will convince the world of sin, and of
righteousness and of judgement . . .

John 16:8

They were cut to the heart and said to Peter, "Brethren,
what shall we do?"

Acts 2:37

The Spirit and the world

First and foremost it is to the Church that the Holy Spirit
is sent, but from there His influence is intended to spill over
powerfully into the world. Jesus made this progression clear
in speaking to His disciples at the Last Supper. He said, "if
I go I will send Him to you." That was the first stage —
the Spirit on the Church. He continued, however, by saying,
"And when he comes he will convince the world . . ." (John
16:8). That was the second stage — the Spirit in the world.

It is impossible to go far in Acts without seeing very clearly
the fulfilment of both of these intentions. The one follows
the other very rapidly. The disciples had barely been filled
with the Holy Spirit on the Day of Pentecost when people
began to gather and Peter found himself preaching to them.
He soon discovered that not only was there a powerful new
dynamic in his own life, but also the Holy Spirit was working
equally powerfully in those who were listening to him. There
was a wide and deep response to his preaching, and three
thousand were converted. All of this is contained in Acts
2 — powerful baptism in the Spirit, powerful preaching,
powerful conviction. They follow in quick succession. It is
a precise model of revival as it has come to be understood.

The history of revivals shows that there is always a very direct connection between these two operations of the Spirit. It is when the Spirit is moving in direct power and anointing on the Church that He moves in powerful conviction amongst unbelievers. The Spirit is one — He empowers and at the same time He convicts. The more room He has for empowering, the more room He has for the work of conviction. It is unthinkable that the Spirit should produce anointings upon preachers and a spirit of witness in the Church and yet not be powerfully working in the hearts of those to whom the preaching and witnessing is directed. It is equally impossible to think of the Spirit acting in the world without being powerfully present in the Church. This has never happened. Both always operate together.

No true revival will be without the dimension of powerful and widespread Holy Spirit conviction in the world. Whilst revival is certainly a time when God moves with great refreshing power on His people, it is also a time when He moves with great conviction upon unbelievers. We can never be satisfied with any concept of revival which does not include powerful impact upon the world. Whether we call the impact on the Church a "revival" and call the impact on the world an "awakening" makes no substantial difference. They are both part of the total effect of the outpouring of the Spirit. Indeed, if the Spirit is not working through the Church in sufficient power to impact the world, He is not in the Church in as full a measure as He should be or seeks to be. If the Church is really unable to impact the world, then however blessed the Church may appear to be, there needs to be an immediate turning to God and a seeking of more of the Spirit.

Empowering on the Church and conviction in the world — that is the Spirit's work in revival. If, therefore, we are thinking seriously towards revival it is important to understand not merely the nature of the empowerings on believers but also the nature of the Spirit's work in conviction. We must fully appreciate how utterly indispensable and fundamental that work of conviction is to any widespread work of conversion. Like an anointing for service, it cannot be worked up or worked out — it can only be prayed down. Moreover, conviction, particularly in revival times, can be a very powerful and overwhelming thing, and we need to learn to distinguish genuine conviction from any counterfeit. We must not be guilty of rejecting the true because of the appearance of the false. Conviction is of crucial importance and must not be misunderstood and rejected.

The nature of conviction

Two simple illustrations will take us straight to the heart of this matter of conviction. Duncan Campbell, writing about the Hebridean Revival, tells the story of a man who one night was watching a moth getting closer and closer to the flame of a candle. This man had no serious thoughts in his mind as he watched the moth. Eventually, however, he found himself saying to the moth, "If you get any closer you will be burned to death." As soon as he had said this he knew it was a parable of his own position before God. He himself was circling the fire of the righteousness of God and he too would be burned once he touched God in eternity. This was no idle thought. He knew it was absolutely true, and he knew that God was speaking directly to him with devastating clarity. He fell on his face, crying out loud for God to have mercy on him. This was no piece of pious acting but an encounter with the eternal God. He had come under conviction.

The second illustration is from Acts and gives some indication of the conviction which was abroad in the early Church. Paul and Silas found themselves in prison at Philippi (Acts 16:25). Despite their lacerated backs they prayed and praised God together well on into the night. An earthquake ripped open the prison doors and set them free. The gaoler broke down before them and demanded to know how he could be saved. They led him to Jesus. The gaoler did not break down because he was afraid the prisoners had escaped: he knew they had not, for Paul told him so. He wanted to know, not how to be saved from his superiors, but how to be saved from the judgement of God. The earthquake on earth had brought him face to face with the judgement that awaited him in the next world. In a moment of time the earthly danger was linked to eternal danger, and judgement became as real as the earthquake. He was greatly under conviction, and he had no hesitation in embracing the faith that had put these two men in prison with bleeding backs. He gladly submitted to baptism at their hands. He had come face to face with the fact of judgement. He had felt the power of conviction through the Spirit in a most extraordinary way.

This, then, is the Spirit's ministry of conviction. It is God getting to the human heart with truth by the Spirit. It is a compelling divine revelation to an unbeliever about the real nature of his state before God. It is not necessarily connected with physical manifestations, though, as we have just seen, these may well happen. It is simply that somewhere deep within a person there is such an inescapable inner conviction concerning spiritual truth that he knows beyond any shadow of doubt that what he is feeling and hearing about his standing before God is absolutely true and real. It is a phenomenon that goes beyond the merely rational. When such conviction falls upon a person, it will make nonsense of rational objection. It is an activity of the Holy Spirit which brings an awareness to the human mind of ultimate truth − truth which cannot be grasped by the intellect alone. It is a communication of spiritual knowledge and spiritual truth in the most profound, authoritative and unmistakable manner. It is truth through conviction, and it is a prime ministry of the Spirit. It is vital that we appreciate and believe in this ministry of the Spirit and pray for it to be powerfully manifested.

It is something that the Spirit alone can do. Man cannot do it. It is fundamental in the salvation of people. Though it cannot be said that such conviction brings an inevitable response of commitment to God, it is an essential step in the process which leads to such commitment. This is true whether we are thinking of revival times or of more normal episodes of Church life. It is something we need to recognise, thoroughly understand and constantly seek after.

Areas of conviction

It is important to notice that when Jesus spoke about this convicting activity of the Spirit in the world, He did not speak merely in general terms but was quite specific about the particular truths that would be so forcibly brought home. He said there would be conviction about three things: sin, righteousness and judgement (John 16:8). Jesus explained that if a person did not believe in Him, he could always be convicted of sin because believing in Him was the only way to get sin removed. Likewise He explained that if a person did not believe in Him he belonged to Satan and therefore could be convicted of the fact that he was under the judgement already pronounced on Satan. Finally He made it clear that relief from these convictions of sin and judgement could only come through a further conviction, namely that He alone could provide the righteousness that was needed. Conviction would, therefore, come upon people who were unbelievers, bringing a sense of guilt, a sense of impending judgement and a recognition that only in Christ could relief be found.

The choice of these three areas indicates very clearly that the convicting activity of the Spirit of God constitutes a work of grace and mercy, not one of judgement. The Spirit brings conviction not for the purpose of condemnation, but rather only for salvation. Conviction of sin and judgement on their own would certainly bring condemnation, for they offer in themselves no spiritual relief. But the Spirit's work of conviction also includes an underlining of the righteousness to be found in Christ, something that provides immediate hope. Thus this activity of the Spirit is not designed to judge, even though those experiencing conviction of sin may well feel themselves to be initially under the severest judgement.

It is intended to show those people their true spiritual state and so to lead them to repentance.

Acts 2 gives us a powerful illustration of the fact that this threefold conviction normally operates through a true and clear preaching of the Gospel. In the plan of God, the Spirit convicts of the truths of which Jesus spoke as those truths are boldly proclaimed. Thus it was that as Peter preached to the assembled crowd conviction fell. In his sermon Peter explained first that what the people were witnessing was the coming of the Spirit, but then he went on to proclaim that the Spirit had come from the Jesus whom they had crucified. He stressed that Jesus was the exalted Lord and Messiah and had truly risen from the dead. As he preached these truths the Holy Spirit brought home to the people the awful reality that Jesus was the Messiah, the righteous One, and that they had committed the worst of sins in rejecting Him. Judgement was inevitable. As a result, cries of deep distress soon rose from the crowd: "What can we do?"

What this episode teaches us is that if we are to expect any real response from the hearts of unbelievers we must seek to preach the very truths about which the Spirit wants to bring conviction. We cannot expect the Spirit to own preaching which is not clearly communicating those truths. The right sort of preaching will, like Peter's sermon, have on the one hand an unshakable insistence on the fact and consequence of sin, and on the other hand a clear presentation of Jesus and what He has done.

This helps us to understand why it is that again and again in times of revival the messages and themes which the Holy Spirit impresses on the hearts of preachers have to do with His holiness. The preaching and the conviction are all of a piece. The much-acclaimed (and by some, much-maligned) sermon by Jonathan Edwards, *Sinners in the hands of an Angry God*, is an obvious example. Preaching with great liberty on that theme, he saw a tremendous wave of conviction move across his hearers, so much so that people actually felt they were literally slipping into hell itself. One onlooker said, "there was great moaning and crying – so the minister was obliged to desist — the shrieks and cries were piercing and amazing". In similar vein, as we have noted before, the preachers of the great 1904 Welsh Revival all felt a strong compulsion to speak on the righteousness of God and the need for holiness.

Not only, however, was the holiness of God central, but so also was the blood and the cross of Jesus. Revival times are times when the sacrifice of Calvary is a theme powerfully on the lips of preachers, for conviction about this truth is as much in the purpose of the Spirit as the other convictions. There is accordingly no room in revival preaching for any weakness concerning either the nature of sin or the power of the blood. Clear affirmation of the truths of sin, judgement and righteousness is what the Spirit demands.

"Cut to the heart" — that was the description of the outworking of the Spirit's ministry of conviction on the Day of Pentecost. It is a strong expression, conveying a deep physical and emotional impact on people. It straight away brings into focus the fact that when the Spirit works during times of revival He works with an extraordinarily deep level of conviction. Conviction is normal to conversion at any time, of course, but the conviction abroad at times of revival is particularly vivid, and frequently produces a deep physical and emotional reaction. Indeed it is this unusually powerful impact of conviction upon unbelievers that has been seen, more than anything else, to typify revival. Attention has perhaps been drawn more to this operation of the Spirit than to any other single factor in revivals. In fact revivals tend to be measured by the extent to which conviction is abroad, both inside and outside the Church. It is as though in considering conviction, we reach into the heart of revival.

A case study in conviction

One of the most influential and informative periods of revival in more modern times was the so-called Great Awakening in the American colonies during the early eighteenth century. It was influential because its central figure, Jonathan Edwards, described and analysed it with great care in his writings. Amongst the large amount of material he produced was a short treatise called *A Narrative of Surprising Conversions*. In this he gave some indication of what happened in New England and the nearby colonies around 1735. It was written to satisfy people in England who were eager to know about the revivings in the colonies. Edwards handled the subject of conviction at length and with great perception, and his thoughts on this matter are as fresh and relevant today as ever they were.

In the course of the *Narrative* he describes in some detail the experience of a lady called Abigail Hutchinson. It is a case study in conviction, designed both to explain and to vindicate such an operation of the Spirit, and it is very instructive. He notes that the starting-point was a remark from her brother about the need of regenerating grace. This caused her to feel she must seek it, and she turned to her Bible. Edwards continues:

> then there came a sudden alteration, by a great increase of her concern, in an extraordinary sense of her own sinfulness, particularly the sinfulness of her *nature*, and wickedness of her heart. This came upon her, as she expressed it, as a flash of lightning, and struck her into exceeding terror . . . Her great terror, she said, was that she had sinned against God: her distress grew more and more for three days; until she saw nothing but blackness and darkness before her, and her very flesh trembled for fear of God's wrath: she wondered and was astonished at herself, that she had been so concerned for her body and had applied so often to physicians to heal that, and had neglected her soul.

She continued reading the Bible, looking for relief, and finding as she did so that all her old trust in "her own prayers and religious performances" were of no comfort. All the time "her sense of her own exceeding sinfulness continued increasing''. She saw more and more clearly that it was not just "sins" but "sin" in her that made her guilty.

> On the Sabbath day she was so ill that her friends thought it best that she should not go to public worship . . . but when she went to bed on the Sabbath night she took up a resolution, that she would the next morning go to the minister. As she awakened on the Monday morning, a little before day, she wondered within herself at the easiness and calmness she felt in her mind, which was of a kind she had never felt before. As she thought of this, such words as these were in her mind: *The words of the Lord are pure words, health to the soul, and marrow to the bones*: and then these words: *The blood of Christ cleanses from all sin*; which were accompanied by a lively sense of the excellency of Christ, and his sufficiency to satisfy for the sins of the whole world . . . By these things her mind was led into such contemplations and views of Christ, as filled her exceeding full of joy.

Edwards relates that she had the same experiences of the presence of Christ on three successive mornings, and that these experiences grew progressively brighter. On the third morning she also felt filled with distress for Christless people and with great love for "all mankind".

Edwards chose to tell this lady's story for a particular reason. He made it quite clear that there was nothing in her temperament or background that tended to "enthusiasm" or ostentation. Yet the depth of her conviction, first of her sin and then of her relief in Christ, was overwhelming. She went through the deepest agonies of soul in coming to recognise her true state of sin and guilt before God. She had a deep awareness of the wrath of God by which judgement would be executed. These were inescapable impressions, producing distinct bodily and mental distress. But she came into immense relief and joy as she saw herself associated with the forgiveness and love of Christ.

For Edwards, there were two very important aspects to

173

this conversion. First, she was convinced not simply of individual sins but of having a heart of sin, and secondly, she came to a point where she realised that there was absolutely no relief to be found in anything she herself might do or offer. Christ alone could meet her need out of pure grace. This was the Spirit's work of conviction going to the very bottom of human need. Edwards saw it as a work which brought a person face to face with the perfect justice of God in His judgement of sinners, and created the recognition that there was no ground whatsoever for forgiveness other than the mercy of God. When these facts were fully grasped, then, and only then, could it be said that a full work had been done in the heart of a sinner. Edwards noted in his *Narrative* some lengthy wrestlings in the hearts of those in whom the Spirit sought to do a complete work of this kind. His own ministry was completely devoted to securing such full and complete conviction.

If this is the depth of the work of the Spirit in revival, it is not surprising, therefore, that there is frequently a peculiar quality about the spiritual life of people who were converted during such times. Nor is it surprising that so many who were thus converted remain solidly and actively Christian. It is a very salutary reminder that revival is not a time of "easy believism" but rather one of deep heart-cleansing and forgiveness. It is a time when the superficial is removed, when sin is sought out and when foundations are properly dug.

In his more general descriptions of the revival, Edwards is careful to point out that there was great variety in the way in which conviction manifested itself amongst people. For some, conviction was a developing process, while for others it came like lightning. Some found relief almost immediately, while others struggled for long periods, trying every kind of self-effort and personal discipline before finding that simple faith was the answer. Some showed every kind of emotional disturbance, while the behaviour of others remained sober and quiet.

An atmosphere of conviction

Speaking more generally of the immense power of conviction of the Spirit that was abroad at the time, Edwards says:

> Persons are sometimes brought to the borders of despair, and it looks as black as midnight to them a little before the day dawns in their souls. Some few instances there have been, of persons who have had such a sense of God's wrath for sin, that they have been overborne; and made to cry out under an astonishing sense of guilt, wondering that God suffers such guilty wretches to live upon the earth, and that he doth not immediately send them to hell.

From time to time this work of conviction would be powerfully seen in open meetings which were reminiscent of Pentecost. Sometimes, after services, "people were so overcome that they could not go home, but were obliged to stay all night where they were". As a certain Jonathan Parsons was preaching at Lyme in 1741, "Many had their countenances changed . . . Great numbers cried out aloud in the anguish of their souls: several stout men fell as though a cannon had been discharged and a ball had made its way through their hearts" (a very pertinent paraphrase of "cut to the heart"!).

So in this Great Awakening we see the essential operations of the Spirit of conviction moving with great power. Before leaving the scene, however, we need to take note of a very important characteristic of this convicting activity: whilst the impact of the Spirit of conviction was intensely individual, there was at the same time the sense of a general conviction abroad. It was, so to speak, "in the atmosphere". Benjamin Trumbull, an historian of the period, writes:

> There was in the minds of people, a general fear of sin, and of the wrath of God denounced against it. There seemed to be a general conviction, that all the ways of man were before the eyes of the Lord. It was the opinion

of men of discernment and sound judgement, who had the best opportunities of knowing the feelings and general state of the people at that period that bags of gold and silver, and other precious things, might with safety, have been laid in the streets, and that no man would have converted them to his own use.[1]

This sort of observation, culled from the numerous eyewitness impressions of the times, throws a good deal of light on two important passages in Acts which in their brevity might all too easily be overlooked or thought insignificant. In Acts 2:43, Luke records that shortly after Peter's preaching on the Day of Pentecost, "fear came upon every soul", and in Acts 5:13 he notes that, when the apostles were in Solomon's Portico after the episode with Ananias and Sapphira, "None of the rest dare join them." Luke is reporting here on a general atmosphere of awe and fear that came to reside at least in certain parts of Jerusalem. F. F. Bruce, in his commentary on Acts, says of the first of those passages, "The conviction of sin that followed Peter's preaching was no momentary panic, but filled the people with a long-lasting sense of awe. This impression was intensified by the wonders and signs which the apostles performed."[2] The second passage clearly indicates the devastating effect which the death of Ananias and Sapphira had on the church in particular: "great fear came upon the whole church". This fear was of such an order that for a time they would not even approach the apostles.

Such awestricken recognition of the presence of God and His power has been noted as a major feature of revival by many who have experienced it. It has sometimes been present throughout a whole community, sometimes felt in some particular geographical locality. At times it has been experienced by unbelievers as they have come into a place where the Gospel was being preached. Speaking of the Hebridean revival, Duncan Campbell was of the opinion that this sense of the pervading and awesome presence of God was the most striking feature he noticed.

Describing the same sort of phenomenon, an eyewitness of the great Ulster Revival of 1859 wrote, "Even upon that portion of the public who make no claim to be religious, a deep solemnizing influence has been exercised. It is like Pentecostal times, when 'fear came upon every soul'." Arthur Wallis writes, "This overwhelming sense of God, bringing deep conviction of sin is perhaps the outstanding feature of true revival." It is in this atmosphere that conversions are thick and fast and the widespread impact on believers is most pronounced. Revival is distinguished by conviction which is not only deep but also widespread.

No one is beyond conviction

One of the most challenging and encouraging features of the ministry of conviction is to be found in the impact it makes on those who seem the most unlikely candidates for conversion. In revival times this impact is very marked. It is through this Holy Spirit activity that the greatest trophies of grace are won.

Let us return once more to the Great Awakening. Jonathan Edwards, at the outset of his *Narrative*, referred euphemistically to a young woman who was "one of the greatest company-keepers" of the town. God had worked in her and had given her a new heart which was truly broken and sanctified. Despite this evident work of grace, Edwards was afraid that her coming into the Church would have a bad effect on people, encouraging them to looseness and hardness. In the event he said, "God made it, I suppose the greatest occasion of awakening to others of any thing that ever came to pass in the town. The news of it seemed to be almost like a flash of lightning upon the hearts of young people all over the town." He was not the first nor the last to be taken by surprise at the sheer depth of the work of the Spirit in the most unlikely hearts. Such converts have an enormous impact on unbelievers.

It is vital to keep a strong expectation that God can and will work on the hardest of hearts. It is precisely for this that we are pleading when we seek God for revival. There is a very great amount of testimony to encourage us in such a hope. John Wesley's and George Whitefield's ministries were constantly accompanied by the presence of a great spirit of conviction, and by extraordinary conversions of the most unlikely people in the most unpromising places. The miners at Kingswood in Bristol were a case in point. They were not touched by Whitefield's oratory, nor by Wesley's solemnity, but the tears ran down their cheeks simply through conviction of sin and conviction of Christ's love. These miners, considered by others in Bristol to be almost animals on account of their violence and uncouthness, were not beyond the awakening of conscience through the Spirit of God.

Wesley also preached from time to time to the "condemned felons in Newgate". On one occasion he preached strongly on the theme that God desires all men to be saved. He reports:

> Immediately one, and then another sank to the earth. They dropped as thunderstruck. One cried aloud. We besought God on her behalf and He turned her heaviness into joy.[3]

All men, of all races, at all times are in this way vulnerable to the conviction of the Spirit of God. Such conviction is the power of God at work and transcends culture and personality. Jonathan Goforth, watching revival break out in Manchuria, was amazed at the power released amongst the Chinese and wrote:

> It is a miracle for stolid, self-righteous John Chinaman to go out of his way to confess sins that no torture of the Yamen could force from him; for a Chinaman to demean himself to crave, weeping, the prayers of his fellow-believers is beyond all human explanation.[4]

His fellow missionaries were equally amazed at the readiness

178

of these proud men to lose face. But they were watching people who were in the grip of conviction and quite incapable of resisting the Spirit. In the Congo a leading evangelist sought out a missionary and confessed to adultery on three occasions. The missionary wrote:

> I saw afresh the truth of what the natives were now saying, the Holy Spirit is making people confess things which they never would have confessed under flogging or torture.[5]

The Africans referred to these moments of conviction as "feeling the whip of the Spirit".

Misunderstanding the outward phenomena of conviction

Not surprisingly, some of the most powerful expressions of the Spirit of conviction have been misunderstood, and have caused both alarm and opposition. The cries and shrieks which were evident in Jonathan Edwards' day and the prostrations which occurred throughout the eighteenth-century revivals have often been repeated in many parts of the world since, and have always met with criticism. They have consistently been seen as expressions of exhibitionism and fleshly excess. Nowhere, perhaps, has this problem raised its head more than in the Ulster Revival of 1859, in which great numbers of people underwent physical reactions to the deepest of convictions. A Presbyterian minister summarised the impact that was felt at that time:

> Through the instrumentality of the Word and prayer, convictions, often the most powerful, even to the *convulsing of the whole frame, the trembling of every joint, intense burning of heart, and complete prostration of strength*, have been produced.[6]

An eminent Belfast minister described what happened at a number of meetings in Antrim:

179

when prayers were addressed to their Lord, strong men became weak, and strong youths fell to the ground; loud cries were uttered, and many tears were shed, and some of those who came to mock cried out for mercy, and remained to pray.

A number of churchmen found the whole thing far too emotional and unbecoming. The medical magazine. the *Lancet* came out violently against the prostrations, calling them dangerous mass hysteria. Those most involved in the revival responded by carefully examining the phenomena and issuing very balanced and helpful statements. No one of repute denied that there were occasions when people could become violently stirred in the flesh, with very little discernible spiritual effect. Most thoughtful observers accepted that such aberrations were likely to happen when God was moving in power. They equally insisted, however, that such fleshly counterfeits were no argument against the reality of true spiritual occurrences. Those of greatest spiritual awareness were never to be found actively encouraging such manifestations, though they were always ready to accept them when they genuinely appeared. A judicious outlook was expressed by a minister from Londonderry, who wrote:

I think about two months ago the prostrations in this place ceased. I don't regret the absence of them. We were glad to take the blessing in any way the God of grace was pleased to bestow it, but the physical sufferings which were evidently the unavoidable accompaniments of the great movement are, in themselves, considered by no means desirable. They were sent by God to serve a special end, and when that purpose was served they ceased. They were sent — in my mind — fully as much for the benefits of others, as for those who were the subjects of them. *Every prostration I firmly believe was a sermon, a thrilling appeal to the profligate and a solemn warning to those who were at ease in Zion.*[7]

John Weir, in his history of the revival, wrote:

> The striking down of the wicked, I was assured by two
> of the town missionaries of Belfast, was the means of
> arresting the attention of the very *worst* of the
> population. On this class of men and women, continued
> persuasions and entreaties had been tried in vain; but
> when one of their number was prostrate before their very
> eyes, when his agony and despair found vent in loud
> cries, they were filled with apprehensions of the reality
> of Divine wrath, of judgement to come and of hell; and
> gathering round the stricken ones they heard — it may
> be for the first time — those gospel statements which,
> applied by the Holy Spirit, brought them to the Saviour's
> feet.

Such comments are a model of the true spiritual discretion
which is ready to accept the extraordinary, without openly
encouraging fleshly excitement and its consequent excess.
Maturity is seen here in the refusal to be pushed away from
true spiritual reality into the unrealities of the over-zealous
and over-emotional.

The bitter accusations of hysteria which issued from the
Lancet were more than adequately met by a number of
observers. They demonstrated clearly that in ordinary life
the sudden presentation of certain truths, such as the news
of the sudden loss of a loved one, could have the most
traumatic effects on people. How much more on certain
people could be the effect of conviction of hell and
judgement! The sudden recognition of such awful truth
through the power of the Spirit understandably caused
people to fall down. At the same time, release through the
acceptance of Christ would bring understandable ecstasies
of joy and praise, of leaping and shouting. Those unable
to appreciate the validity of this argument were, of course,
in the main those who were unable to accept the fact that
conviction by the Spirit was conviction about the real facts
of eternity. This conviction and the reaction it caused were

disparagingly dubbed the results of "enthusiasm", a term which at that time had abusive connotations.

Conviction in the Church

The emphasis of this chapter has been on conviction amongst those who are in the world, because that was the emphasis which Jesus Himself stressed. That does not mean, however, that conviction is not to be found in the Church. The fact is that all too often the world is to be found in the Church, and wherever the world is to be found conviction of sin, and indeed judgement, will follow. For many, indeed, the mention of revival brings to mind first and foremost a radical movement of conviction amongst indifferent, worldly and sinful Christians. If we turn, for example, to the revival in Ruanda in East Africa, it is the burning flame of holiness moving amongst an almost nominal church that stands out above all else. In Congo, some years later, it was the same. The leaders in particular were so searched by the Spirit that adulteries, thefts and even murders were being openly confessed. Again and again on the mission field this has been the story. The Church has lapsed so badly into gross, pagan sin that powerful moves of the Spirit have been required for it to be brought back into any resemblance of true Christianity.

We must concede that the pathway to a revival activity of conviction in the world will always be found in a great work of conviction within the hearts of God's people. This is where revival always starts. When conviction has burned away the dross in the lives of the saints, then and only then will it begin to burn powerfully in the world. That is something we need to be ready for!

Whether it is in the Church or amongst unbelievers, however, this activity of the Spirit in bringing conviction is one of the most compelling facts which calls us to seek God for a revival. This is what revival is all about. It is what we are praying for. Again and again in revivals large numbers of people have been mown down by the "scythe" of the convicting Spirit. Brainerd saw it amongst the Indians, Finney saw it amongst Americans and Europeans, Goforth saw it amongst the Chinese, Rees Howell saw it amongst the Africans. A whole host of others have seen it. We may endeavour to have the same sort of conviction in our own churches, especially through preaching, but essentially it is something which comes only in answer to believing prayer.

Notes

1. Quoted by Iain Murray, *Jonathan Edwards*, p. 167.
2. F. F. Bruce, *Commentary on Acts* (New London Series).
3. John Wesley, *Journal*.
4. J. Gosforth, *By My Spirit*, p. 17.
5. *This is That*, anonymous CLC publication. This small, powerful testimony is full of illustrations of conviction at work in the most powerful of ways.
6. John Weir, *Heaven Came Down*. This book contains a great deal of hand testimony from ministers who were personally involved in the revival of 1859. Conviction is a very marked feature in their reports.
7. Ibid. The book (especially Part III) includes detailed discussion about the debate over the physical phenomena which accompanied conviction.

Chapter 11: Numerical Impact

And more than ever believers were added to the Lord, multitudes both of men and women.

Acts 5:14 (RSV)

"Revival and conversions cannot be dissociated. They go together. Whenever the church experiences Pentecost, conversions invariably ensue." So wrote Arthur Skevington Wood, the Methodist historian, introducing a chapter on John Wesley. It is a true statement, and we could go on to add that in times of revival there have not only been conversions, but a very great many of them. In fact one of the most significant characteristics of revival has been the immense spiritual harvests that have been reaped. Indeed, to many, it is the large-scale conversion of unbelievers that has been the crowning glory of revival.

We need to be absolutely sure that we never allow this aspect of revival to grow dim in our prayer and faith. If we take Acts as our guide and allow it to inform our vision we shall certainly avoid that danger, because it is quite impossible to turn to Acts without being confronted on almost every page with a panorama of very large number of people becoming Christians. Luke is constantly bringing before us descriptions of large gatherings of people listening to the preaching of the Gospel, and he records that as a result there is a remarkable numerical growth in the Church. If Acts underlines anything about revival, it is this factor of the extraordinary numbers that gather to hear the Gospel and respond to it.

It is an aspect which, I believe, we must constantly reflect on and allow to become part of our vision. God's promise, purpose and desire is for a "multitude which no man can number", and revivals are mighty times of harvesting in the process of fulfilling that plan. We must be interested in numbers, because God is. For every single individual in a crowd is, after all, a person.

Acts — church growth *par excellence*!

To return, then, to Acts. The picture it paints is without any question something quite extraordinary. Not only did the Day of Pentecost see people so deeply wounded with conviction that they felt physically stabbed in the heart, but it saw also no fewer than 3,000 so affected, and all at one and the same time. It was a day of brokenness and loud cries amongst the crowds. We are not told how many were present in total to hear Peter on that day. The figure of 3,000 refers only to the people who responded immediately to the conviction they felt. There may well have been a great many more than that listening to Peter, and many may have responded to his pleas at a later stage. Whatever the size of the crowd, the fact is that the Holy Spirit made a devastating impact on the hearers.

The first dramatic ingathering on the Day of Pentecost was, of course, only the beginning. It was not unique. It was followed immediately by a constant and daily stream of additions to the Church as a great outbreak of personal witness and apostolic preaching swept across Jerusalem (Acts 2:47). The crowds were soon back to hear Peter preach again after the cripple was healed at the Beautiful Gate, and it looks very much as though a further 5,000 were added as a result (Acts 4:4).[1] The sense of awe and the power of conviction grew as the days went by, largely because of the miracles worked by the apostles.[2] Luke records that "more than ever believers were added to the Lord, multitudes both of men and women". It seems as though there came a point when it was no longer possible to count the thousands who were responding. The impact was clearly one that affected all Jerusalem, for the High Priest accused the apostles with the words, "you have filled Jerusalem with your teaching . . ." (Acts 5:28). Luke summed up the situation by saying that "the number of disciples in Jerusalem increased rapidly". Significantly, he was able to add that it was not just ordinary people who became disciples, but also "a large number of priests became obedient to the faith" (Acts 6:7).

Jerusalem was literally stirred from end to end. Thousands of people became Christians, despite the intense opposition of the authorities. We shall never know exactly how many were converted, but the expressions used in Acts could well indicate some tens of thousands. Astonishingly, all of it had sprung out of a mere hundred and twenty souls clinging to a promise in prayer, and it had all happened within a matter of a few weeks.[3] It was a most amazing turning of the tables. Calvary had seemed to be a defeat, but now God was utterly triumphant. This was the unmistakable revelation of the sovereign power of the Holy Spirit, who was now engaged in a huge reaping of souls. That, however, is the revival model. That is the powerful challenge to faith that springs from the pages of Acts.

We should be quite wrong, however, if we thought that the picture which Acts gives us of numerical impact ends in Jerusalem. The revival streams in fact poured out far beyond the city, and with results that were perhaps even more astonishing to the original disciples. When persecution in Jerusalem scattered the newly formed Church, Philip began to preach in Samaria, and he found that "the crowds paid close attention to what he said" (Acts 8:6). The important word here is "crowds". Very large numbers gathered together to hear him, and very large numbers were affected. The impact on the people was so great that the city's chief sorcerer, a man of great occult power, was overthrown. The city was permeated with joy and the presence of the Spirit. Luke sums up what happened with these words: "Samaria accepted the word of God" (Acts 8:14). Large numbers of Jews being converted was one thing,

186

but the conversion of large number of Samaritans was astonishing!

God had more surprises in store. While Philip went to Samaria to preach, others went much farther north and eventually came to Antioch of Syria. Acts contains no accounts of desperate struggles to survive in this very different Gentile and cosmopolitan culture. On the contrary, Luke tells us that once again "The Lord's hand was with them, and a great number of people believed and turned to the Lord" (Acts 11:21). Moreover, when Barnabas joined them at Antioch some time later the power of God was still moving, and after he arrived "a great number of people were brought to the Lord" (Acts 11:24). The result was a church so big that even Barnabas could not handle it, and he brought Paul from Tarsus to help him. Together they taught "great numbers of people" (Acts 11:26).[4]

The dynamic that had produced the Antioch church made it in its turn a powerful missionary church, and the two chief leaders, Paul and Barnabas, were sent out to yet more Gentile areas. So much is common knowledge. What is not always so clearly appreciated is that as they went out the Spirit of revival went with them. We read that when they reached the other Antioch (Antioch of Pisidia), although their first Sabbath's preaching was quiet enough, on "the next Sabbath almost the whole city gathered together to hear the word of God" (Acts 13:44). They moved on to Iconium and "they spoke so effectively that a great number of Jews and Gentiles believed" (Acts 14:1). Shortly afterwards they were at Derbe, and "won a large number of disciples" (Acts 14:21). Paul went back some time later to revisit these cities, and found that the churches were growing in numbers daily (Acts 16:5). For a whole decade this went on (*circa* AD 50-60), and wherever Paul went large and powerful churches sprang up. At Corinth, for example, he was told personally by the Lord Himself, "I have many people in this city" (Acts 18:10), and so it proved to be. At Ephesus, where a wholesale turning away from magic and the occult took place, "the word of the Lord spread widely and grew in power'' (Acts 19:20). Moreover, in a number of places, such as Philippi, churches sprang up in the face of the most bitter persecution.

What all this amounts to is that the same powerful surge of the Spirit that was evident in the beginning at Jerusalem was still evident some thirty years later in many other cities and districts. In those places it was still the same story of conviction of sin on a wide scale, of large crowds gathering to hear the Word of God, and rapid growth. How else can we explain the emergence of such a widespread and thriving Christian community across the Mediterranean world?

Acts repeated in history

Scepticism (from whatever source) concerning this kind of numerical growth cannot be allowed to push this sort of Holy Spirit activity into obscurity. We have to face the fact that the Book of Acts is not the only place where this sort of account may be read. There are many such chapters in the record of Christian history, and there are many such chapters being written in our own generation. Such numerical surges are the stuff of revival. They need to be constantly looked at, and the challenge they present needs to be constantly faced.

J. Edwin Orr has contributed a great deal to our knowledge of the revivals of the last two centuries, and nowhere is his research more careful or thorough than in the area of numerical impact. One of his first major study contributions was to survey the great revivals of 1858–60. These revivals began in the United States in 1858 and eventually moved on to Ulster, Wales, Scotland and England. The revival in America ''swept every state'', and Orr computes that over a million converts were added to the churches.[5] The population of the States was 31 million at that time,[6] and only about 5 million of those people had clear Christian commitment. So this revival movement had an enormous impact, one in every twenty-five of the uncommitted being converted in about two years.[7]

The details of such a movement make fascinating reading. Orr, writing about the events in New York, draws attention to the prayer meeting started by Lamphier in September 1857. This grew within six months into a prayer movement in which 10,000 met daily, filling several of the largest auditoriums in the city. Orr goes on, "Before very long, 10,000 New Yorkers had been converted to God and were in the care of the churches, and in May a good authority gave the total for the city as 50,000 converts."[8] This, of course, was only the spring of the first year of that great movement of the Spirit. In the following months this flood of conversions continued in New York and rapidly spread elsewhere across the States. It was impossible, it seems, to keep pace with the numbers:

A Baptist journal attempted to keep abreast of the news of conversions reaching its office, but its editor apparently gave up the task after listing 17,000 conversions reported to him by Baptist leaders in three weeks.[9]

Summing up, Orr says:

the influence was felt everywhere in the nation. It first captured the great cities, but it also spread through every town and village and country hamlet. It swamped schools and colleges. [Yale experienced an awakening in which it was impossible to estimate the conversions.[10]] It affected all classes without respect to condition . . . the number of conversions reported soon reached the total of 50,000 weekly, a figure borne out by the fact that church statistics show an average of 10,000 additions to church membership weekly for the period of two years[11]

This kind of information, the result of painstaking research for an Oxford Doctorate,[12] is a plain factual confirmation of the revival phenomenon with which Acts challenges us. That phenomenon, in which thousands were brought to Christ, was not a picture conjured up by some second-century imaginative idealist. It was the actual result of an outpouring of the Holy Spirit, an outpouring carefully researched by Luke in his own day and providentially preserved for us.

The phenomenon of the gathering crowds

It is worth looking more carefully at the large crowds that are consistently drawn to listen to the preaching of the Gospel in revival times. The first crowds that gathered in the apostolic revival did so at the Temple in Jerusalem. It was the biggest place in the city. It was the place for rich and poor alike. It was a natural meeting place, and it became the scene of daily preaching and teaching to ever-increasing numbers. The annals of revival are full of examples of very large numbers of people being drawn together to hear the Gospel proclaimed. Such gatherings are a clear feature of revival and they indicate that a kind of divine magnetism is at work.

When revival swept through London in 1860 the poor flocked not into the "temples" but into the theatres. The best and biggest were taken over for some two years as the preachers of that generation proclaimed the Gospel week in and week out to vast congregations. Seven theatres, including well-known ones such as the Garrick and Sadler's Wells, were thrown open every Sunday evening in the early months of 1860 for services, "attracting overwhelming and immense audiences to hear sermons from both Established clergymen and Dissenting ministers". By the spring the aggregate attendance at these services was more than 20,000. These meetings were co-ordinated by a committee under the chairmanship of Lord Shaftesbury and were intended specifically to reach "the unchurched masses of London". Orr reveals how very quickly other theatres were taken over by other groups. Richard Weaver took the Victoria Theatre, for example, and over a four-year period had a total attendance of 865,000 people. Special meetings were opened up in the East End, and there were "numberless free special services in and around London". Orr states: "On the basis of known figures alone, it can be safely said that some 50,000 of London's unchurched people were reached each Sunday in the theatre services or *a million aggregate each season during the revival.*"

If the theatres were the main centres, the "temples" were not entirely neglected! The great cathedrals of London were involved to a degree rarely seen before or since. Orr tells us that "Special services were held in St Paul's Cathedral and Westminster Abbey." Also, "Vast but orderly crowds attended St Paul's." Though there are no statistics available for these revival services, Orr is of the opinion that on the basis of sitting space and reports of crowded gatherings, an estimate of 100,000 aggregate "would be modest".[13]

These astonishing scenes of unprecedented crowds hearing the Gospel in London were matched by many similar scenes across the British Isles. Ballymena, one of the first towns in Ireland to feel the impact of the revival, had a population of about 6,000 and witnessed a spontaneous meeting of some 5,000 in a nearby quarry. When, later, the evangelist Brownlow North appeared, the same town was the scene of a Sunday open air meeting of 11,000 people as well as some crowded church services. Elsewhere in Ireland, Brownlow North attracted 2,000 people to a meeting in a town of 900 individuals. The numbers of those attending subsequent meetings in that town grew steadily to 7,000 and some 300 out of the 900 resident townsfolk were converted. Another great contemporary evangelist, Grattan Guinness, preached to at least 15,000 people in the open air at Belfast and a further 6,000 at Coleraine. The revival in Scotland began with a meeting of some 20,000 people "crushing and pushing to hear the speakers" on Glasgow Green one evening in August 1860. In the same month, in Perth, 4,000 people were addressed by fifty pastors and lay preachers for seven hours.[14]

These scenes were not just isolated and few and far between. There were very few towns in Britain that did not witness large crowds and large numbers of conversions.

191

It all amounted to a result very similar to that of the 1859 Revival in America: one million people joined the evangelical churches; 100,000 were converted in Wales, 100,000 in Ulster, 300,000 in Scotland and 600,000 in England.

Though very different in some respects from this great revival movement of the nineteenth century, the revivals of the eighteenth century were still characterised by the gathering together of large crowds. When Whitefield was in London he invariably drew together enormous numbers of people. On more than one occasion, for example, an estimated crowd of 40,000 assembled on Hampstead Heath. That may have been exceptional even for Whitefield, but there are numerous references in both his journal and that of John Wesley to meetings in the capital attended by at least tens or twenties of thousands. The meeting places for these sort of gatherings were, of course, the fields, though again and again we read also of large congregations in the churches and halls.

As was the case in the 1860s, these extraordinary gatherings of people took place all over the country. Bristol was a major centre of activity, and typical of Whitefield's visits to Bristol are the following extracts:

Sunday at 4, I hastened to Kingswood. There were about ten thousand to hear me . . .

On Sunday, March 4, I went to Newgate and preached to an exceedingly large congregation. I then hastened to Hannam Mount, three miles from the city, where the coal miners all live. Over four thousand were ready to hear me . . . at four in the afternoon I went to the mount on Rose Green and preached to over fourteen thousand. So good was my God that all could hear.

On Sunday 19, I was enabled to go and preach at Hannam to many more than were there last Sunday. In the afternoon I really believe no less than twenty thousand were present at Rose Green.

This eighteenth-century movement was different to the one in the 1860s in that the large gatherings were part of very long ministries and were spread over several decades, not merely two years. Whitefield preached his first sermon at the age of twenty-one, and the power in his preaching was immediately apparent. He died thirty-four years later, having preached throughout that period ten and sometimes twenty times a week to very large crowds in all parts of the country. If we were to aggregate the numbers of those who heard the Gospel from his lips over those years we should have some very remarkable figures indeed. One such computation estimated that he preached 18,000 sermons to over 10 million people. If we added to that a similar aggregate for John Wesley and other contemporaries, the total would amount to virtually a whole nation!

The hand of God at work

It is important that we recognise that the gathering together of such huge crowds of people to hear and respond to the Gospel was not the result of human organisation or evangelistic planning. It was a direct operation of the Holy Spirit. While there must never be a time in the life of the Church when it is not seeking to proclaim the Gospel to all and sundry, there must never be such an exclusive concentration on human activity that no thought is given to the extraordinary difference that a powerful move of the Holy Spirit can and does make. In His power more can be done in a day than in many years of human effort.

Humanly speaking, there was no real reason why the miners of Bristol should have turned out in their thousands to hear either Whitefield or Wesley. Neither was there any reason why they should have listened to them often for one or two hours at a time, and with great solemnity. These were remarkable and very extraordinary times when the power of the Spirit was greatly at work. When a window has to be removed in a parish church because there are more people in the churchyard than in the building and all are clamouring to hear the preacher, then something very powerful is happening.[15] At such times God is among the crowds, calling them, compelling them and powerfully working His conviction upon them.

The twentieth century's vindication of Acts

Though the eighteenth and nineteenth centuries hold some remarkable instances of numerical gains for the Church of God through revival, there is really no question at all that it is our own century which has produced the largest crowds and the most astonishing numerical growth in the history of the Church. Apart from the early years of this century, this growth has not taken place in Britain and North America, the traditional areas of revival. Instead the growth has happened in Asia, Africa, South America and other former mission fields of the world. It has been a century of sweeping revivals, and it has been the sovereign dynamic of the Holy Spirit which has drawn the crowds in the most amazing of ways and reaped millions of converts from them.

The South American revival movements, to take one area, have produced mass meetings and numerical results which certainly put the harvests depicted in Acts into the category of firstfruits and dwarf the revivals of earlier eras. Some simple figures clearly show the magnitude of the Spirit's impact. In the 1940s there were 2 million evangelical Christians in South America. By the 1950s this figure had more than doubled and had reached 5 million, and by the 1960s it had doubled yet again and stood at 10 million. The 1970s saw enormous growth as yet another doubling took place, and 10 million more were added – one million converts for each year of the decade![16]

During each of those decades great crowds were drawn to hear the preaching of the Gospel. Tommy Hicks' visit to Argentina in 1954 gained the goodwill of President Peron and secured the largest stadiums in the country. When powerful healings were witnessed at Hicks' meetings the daily attendance rapidly escalated to 100,000 and eventually to 240,000. An unprecedented and most significant breakthrough for evangelical preaching was secured. One effect of this was a tenfold increase in the number of Pentecostal churches over ten years.

The sixties began with Billy Graham preaching to 200,000 at the Maracana Stadium in Rio de Janeiro, Brazil. An independent Pentecostal, Manoel de Melo, began to preach in the parks of Sao Paulo to crowds of 100,000 and 200,000. De Melo saw vast numbers of people converted, and he set out to build a 25,000-seat auditorium. The work (called Brazil for Christ) grew with amazing rapidity and had congregations totalling 100,000 by the end of the sixties, and 240,000 by the mid-seventies.[17] All over the Latin American countries there was a forthright evangelistic thrust involving many thousands of people. It betokened a most powerful move of the Spirit. There have also been enormous crowds in many other countries across the world. For example, in Korea was seen the first-ever crowd of 1 million.

Though such large-scale preaching has been a clear mark of revival times, amazing numerical growth can none the less actually take place where, for one reason or another, it is not possible to gather such crowds. It seems that in those situations the Holy Spirit simply draws people to a vast number of smaller meetings. Modern day movements of the Spirit in Eastern Europe, Russia and China have seen something of this phenomenon. The extraordinary revivals which have taken place in China, particularly in the late eighties, are very much a case in point. Estimates vary, but it seems there have been at the very least some 25 million conversions to Christ in China — and all in the face of adamant political opposition. This appears to constitute the greatest revival episode the world has yet seen, even though large-scale meetings have been impossible. One of the main human instruments of this revival has been the travelling evangelist who at great cost and with great commitment has kept one step ahead of the secret police. It seems that great crowds and great personalities are not part of the scene.

The phenomenon of mass conversion

The Book of Acts is a story of extraordinary church growth. A particularly challenging episode in that story is the very simple and short account of Peter's visit to Lydda, a town some twenty miles north-west of Jerusalem. At first glance it seems a very ordinary episode. However, the text says quite bluntly, "all those who lived in Lydda and Sharon . . . turned to the Lord" (Acts 9:35). Lydda was a fair-sized town, while Sharon seems to have been a district around it. The claim here is that "*all* those who lived there" were converted. Luke is not loose in his terminology. When he wants to say that there were many converts, he uses the word "many" − in fact he does just this later in the chapter when describing events in Joppa (Acts 9:42). When he says that "all" were converted, he means precisely that. In other words, we have here in Acts a claim of a whole township and even a whole area being converted!

This sort of claim, all too easily dismissed as unthinkable, turns out to be a true pointer to the kind of thing that God has been doing in our own generation. This wholesale conversion of communities is a well-documented phenomenon in many parts of the world, particularly where there are close-knit social units of one kind or another. A recent report out of China provides an amazing example. In a certain mountainous area of that country a pastor was imprisoned, leaving behind him 170 believers. Twenty-two years later he was released, and found that the number of believers had grown to 5,000. Two and half years later there were 56,000 Christians in that area, which had a total population of 60,000. Such figures indicate that whole villages must have come over to Christ.[18]

196

Other reports from China confirm this "people movement" activity of the Holy Spirit. Arthur Wallis tells of one commune of 10,000 which is totally Christian and of an incredible people movement in the province of Honan: "With a population of seventy million, astounding numbers have been turning to the Lord, whole villages and production teams at a time. In one county it is estimated that the Christians number 300,000 out of a population of 700,000." He goes on to quote a comment made by Leslie Lyall: "in some rural areas over 90 per cent of the population are Christian . . . a totally unprecedented statistic in the history of the Church in China".[19]

China is, of course, a land of strong family ties and has a powerful sense of community. This makes it precisely the sort of place where this kind of movement might happen. This does not make the response merely cultural and nominal, however, for what actually takes place is a mass individual response to the Gospel. The conversions are genuine. Wherever such movements take place, this is evident. Donald McGavran, the pioneer of church growth studies, gives the following account, which shows the true spiritual depth of such mass conversions:

> When the 8,000 Dani tribesmen in West New Guinea declared for Christ, they resolved to burn their fetishes on a given day. This symbolic act destroyed their former fears and allegiances and opened the way for them to learn biblical truth. Then, in one of the Indonesian Islands, twenty Moslem communities decided to accept Christ and turn their mosques into churches . . . Participating in such a decision required genuine personal faith.[20]

It is interesting that far from seeing this kind of phenomenon as rare and unusual, McGavran is of the opinion that two-thirds of all converts in Asia, Africa and Oceania have come to Christ through people movements, whether small or great.

197

The challenge of scepticism

When Jonathan Edwards found himself in the middle of a move of God which was affecting a very large proportion of the inhabitants of his town (300 people were converted out of just 200 families), he found himself very reluctant to publicise it, despite the many who were pressing him to do so. The reason for his reluctance was, in his own words, simply this: "I am very sensible, how apt many would be, if they should see the account I have given here, presently to think that I am very fond of making a great many converts, and of magnifying the matter." In other words, this very precise, accurate and sober man was well aware of the fact that the magnitude of what had happened was such that an account of it would meet with a great deal of scepticism.[21]

Edwards was right. Many opposed and found fault. Sadly, that so often happens when the extent of God's working by the Spirit is reported. Scepticism is a common response in such situations. People's minds become so touched by the rational and normal that they look upon anything which is other than rational as exaggeration. Scepticism can also spring out of prejudice, especially where growth is connected with spiritual activity which does not fit into someone's own theological framework. Peter Wagner's very honest description of his own pilgrimage through that sort of prejudice makes fascinating reading.[22] Scepticism can spring too out of the sheer apprehension that the challenge of an unknown spiritual dimension can bring to an already struggling heart.

The fact is, however, that when we come to look carefully at the sheer numbers that have been involved in revival movements, substantiated by those who have sought to provide as great a degree of accuracy as possible, we are brought face to face with a phenomenon which is only too real and which is utterly inexplicable except on the basis of an outpouring of the Spirit. Nothing else explains either the extraordinary magnetism that draws great crowds to hear the preaching of the Gospel or the large numbers who come under conviction and respond in faith.

Whilst such a possibility is held out to us, no matter how earnestly we may work with what we have in any present situation, there must always be a heart and an eye toward these greater things that God can do. I am very much of the opinion that in these days of increasingly vast numbers, even the most efficient and the most sincere attempts to gather in the harvest simply will not be sufficient for the task. The harvest is so great that only the Great Reaper, the Spirit, working in great power, is sufficient. That is undoubtedly the lesson to be learned from the twentieth century.

Postscript

The very large additions that were part and parcel of the revival movement in Acts present an obvious and very pertinent question. How were such overwhelming numbers integrated into the Christian community and properly discipled? What structures carried such numbers and how were they developed?

This really calls for an exhaustive study, but it might be useful to list a number of pointers from the narrative of Acts.

1. There was no way in which the 120 could have laid any plans to cope with the thousands that were to be added to the Church. They could scarcely have expected such developments. They certainly did not hold back from the clear commission to witness on account of the possible problems of integration that might follow. Neither did the Spirit of God. When the revival came, God already had His strategy.

2. The 3,000 converted on the Day of Pentecost, along with those converted "daily", met first in the Temple, where they listened to the preaching and teaching of the apostles and

worshipped together. This was essential, because the apostles alone held the teaching that they required. The apostles perhaps taught *in rota* at length over a fairly prolonged time. The Temple was a large, public concourse ideally suited for this. It appears that the believers still kept the Jewish "hours of prayer" (Acts 3:1 etc.). In addition, it is clear that they also met in their homes, a more intimate setting where doubtless discussions concerning their new faith took place (2:46; 5:42). The homes also became the place for earnest and prolonged prayer (12:12). The Christians of course owned no buildings throughout this period, and indeed well beyond it.

3. In all this the converts were doing things which were not new to them. The patterns developing were ones with which they, as Jews, were familiar. They were perfectly accustomed to meeting centrally in the Temple and to meeting in the home. The Passover family feast was an example of the latter. They also had the pattern of the synagogue to follow. There were, therefore, well-defined ways in which they could organise themselves as a community. The Jewish social culture was rapidly adapted.

4. Cohesion in the Church was obtained by a number of factors. First, the authority of the apostles was clearly undisputed: their teaching and the signs which followed them left people in awe of them. Secondly, there was a very powerful spirit of love and mutual help abroad (Acts 2:44) which undoubtedly acted as a strong spiritual cement, bonding believers together. Persecution would have had the same effect. So there would have been great unity, even if it were strained at times by growth, e.g. 6:1ff. Thirdly, the role of "elders" and the concept of authority were very much a part of the culture.

5. The provision of tutored leadership would doubtless have been a problem. This is the crucial demand at times of rapid growth. The narrative, however, indicates that many people

of considerable gifts were quickly raised up (e.g. the seven deacons of Acts 6). Also, we should remember that many people in Jerusalem and Judea at that time would have already had some Christian teaching. Jesus had spent some two to three years giving thorough and widespread teaching about the Kingdom, both in Jerusalem and Galilee. What was being taught by the apostles was not entirely new to many ears. Moreover, there was a good base of biblical knowledge among the converts which would be rapidly reinterpreted in the light of the new perspective.

6. Thus in the subculture of the Jews there were many factors which allowed structures to develop effectively and rapidly. The real moulding factor was obviously the extremely powerful spiritual impetus that was bringing so many people into fellowship.

7. It is worth noting that the worst problems in discipling arose in the Gentile churches. Corinth was particularly difficult, and pagan behaviour very evident there. Most churches in the Gentile world would seem, however, to have included a proportion of Jewish converts, who might have brought some stability. This shows us the great value of the presence of people who at conversion already have some basic knowledge of God and His ways.

8. Though the apostolic outpouring, occurring in the context of the Jewish subculture of the day, happened in a setting in which there were factors favourable to its development, we in our own generation should not be afraid of rapid development and the conversion of large numbers of people. God still works in the "fullness of time" and makes preparation. On the other hand, preparation for revival must include the most diligent teaching and instructing of large numbers of Christians in vital truth and leadership, for nothing can be left to chance.

Notes

1. It is possible to see the 5,000 not as the number of additional converts but as the total number of those affected up to that point. Whichever interpretation we adopt, we are talking about thousands of converts.
2. The effect of sign and wonder is considered in Chapter 12.
3. The narrative of Acts gives no clear time scale. If the events started in AD 29, then some three years elapsed between then and the time when Paul was converted. The overall impression, however, from the early chapters is one of a rapidly expanding work, and we are left feeling that within a mere matter of weeks some thousands of people became Christians. But it may be the case that we are watching extraordinary growth over a two- to three-year period in Jerusalem.
4. Paul must have been in Antioch towards the end of the AD 40s. It is difficult to say how long the work at Antioch had been going on at that point. One gets the impression that Barnabas had not been in Antioch for a long period before he fetched Paul, and doubtless Barnabas would have been despatched from Jerusalem as soon as the work in Antioch reached a significant stage. We may be looking at a rapid growth, therefore, from about AD 45, though the first conversions could well have taken place as early as AD 35.
5. Edwin Orr, *Second Evangelical Awakening*, p. 5.
6. Ibid., p. 35.
7. Ibid., p. 17.
8. Ibid., p. 20.
9. Ibid., p. 20.
10. Ibid., p. 23.
11. Ibid., p. 21.
12. Ibid., p. 9.
13. Ibid., ch. 5.
14. Ibid., chs. 2 and 3.
15. An event described in Whitefield's Journal.
16. Edwin Orr, *Evangelical Awakenings in Latin America*, p. 169.
17. Ibid., chs. 19 and 20.
18. Ross Paterson, *Heartcry for China*, p. 163.
19. Arthur Wallis, *China Miracle*, pp. 101–110.

20. Donald McGavran, quoted by R. Pointer in *Why Churches Grow*, p. 38.
21. Jonathan Edwards, *Narrative of Surprising Conversions*, Concluding Remarks.
22. See Peter Wagner, *Spiritual Power and Church Growth*, p. 13.

*The Lord gave witness to the word of his grace,
granting signs and wonders to be done by their
hands.*

Acts 14:3

*. . . grant to your servants to speak your word
with all boldness, while you stretch out your hand
to heal, and signs and wonders are performed
through the name of your holy servant Jesus.*

Acts 4:29–30

Chapter 12: Sign and Wonder

Now many signs and wonders were done among the people by the hands of the apostles.

Acts 5:12

Facing the fact of sign and wonder

Ross Paterson, speaking about late-1980s China in his book *Heart Cry for China*, makes the following statement:

> Healings, miracles, signs and wonders are the norm for Christians in China. They are not taken completely by surprise when people are raised from the dead, delivered from evil spirits or healed of all kinds of diseases. They do not read books and teaching material telling them how to get into this kind of ministry, for they preach it as part of their everyday life in Christ.[1]

This extremely moving report, backed up by many others from the same part of the world, once more emphasises a fact that has been thrust upon us many times, namely that when God is moving powerfully by His Spirit in revival, signs and wonders can become a perfectly "natural" part of the process. What is more, they are generally received with quiet faith and heartfelt joy by those who witness them and benefit by them. What a proliferation there now is of testimony to sign and wonder, and from all over the world! The only note of sadness about it, perhaps, is that the main weight of it seems to come from non-Western countries — though at the same time one feels a sense of profound thankfulness that God has been so powerfully at work in this particular way in the so-called "mission field" areas of the world.

Accounts of this nature will come as no surprise, of

course, to those who are ready to allow the Book of Acts to give some forewarning, illumination and guidance about what the Spirit can and might do. The testimony of Acts concerning sign and wonder is abundantly plain for all to see. It demonstrates to us that when God poured out the Holy Spirit on the early Church, signs and wonders and what we call the "supernatural" simply became an integral part of the flow of blessing. Accounts of such happenings are written on page after page of the book, very much as they are in the gospels. It is evident that the early Church was not in the least stumbled by such manifestations (though perhaps it was at times surprised by them!). They readily accepted them, with a thankfulness appropriately tinged with awe. Moreover, the early Christians were sufficiently aware of the power and potential of such manifestations as to deliberately, specifically and earnestly pray for them to happen (Acts 4:30)! They were not so much the subject of theological and psychological investigation (edifying though that undoubtedly can be) as the subject of praise and prayer. Those early Christians unashamedly wanted them!

How different this attitude is to that which has generally pervaded the Western world over the decades of this century. There has been a persistent rejection of the testimony of Acts as a relevant guide to contemporary supernatural manifestations of the Spirit. Even now, as we come to the last decade of this century, this rejection is still hovering about us. These days it is not so much in the form of dogmatic theological statements of denial but is rather in the form of indefinable, but very real, negative attitudes toward the idea of God working through sign and wonder. Although such divine activity is increasingly being recognised as biblically authenticated, there is still a tendency to disparage it or to stand aloof from it.

Reluctance to accept sign and wonder

What were those signs and wonders which the apostles experienced? On the Day of Pentecost itself they heard a mighty rushing wind, they saw visions of tongues of fire and then spoke in other tongues. These signs were, of course, right at the forefront of the coming of the Spirit, and so, in a sense, signs and wonders were in at the start! They were not afterthoughts.

Looking for a moment at that first great sign — the rushing wind which heralded the Spirit — are we to take the view that, in reading Acts, we are only surveying the occurrence of interesting but non-repeatable spiritual phenomena? What, then, should be make of the following?

On August 27th, 1970, Muri Thompson, preaching at Sifolo in the Solomon Islands called for a time of silent prayer. In the hush that followed he heard a sound. "At first," he said, "I thought it was audible prayer among the congregation, but realised that it was above, in the distance, like a wind, and getting louder. I looked up through an opening in the leaf roof to the heavens from which the sound seemed to be coming. It grew to a roar — then it came to me: surely this is the Holy Spirit coming like a mighty rushing wind."

The church building stood at the foot of a very steep hill. While the service was going on three of the leaders of the church were praying in a small house on the hillside. They noticed that the congregation below had fallen silent.

Then they heard the noise: it was not everywhere — it was just immediately above the church. George Strachan, inside the church, at first dismissed the sound as being an airplane far away. But as he came closer he thought, "Is it a gale blowing up?" . . . he looked out to see if the trees were moving — but their leaves were perfectly still. Then he thought, "This is the Holy Spirit coming as at Pentecost."

In a matter of minutes the silent church began to echo with wailing, praying and strong crying. As the leaders gave praise aloud, cries of conviction among the people increased. Gradually they started to come through to deliverance . . . no pain . . . all under the control of God.[2]

Faced with this kind of testimony, are we to say that any form of supernatural manifestation, even if it looks like something in Acts, must be satanic or delusion? Are we to surrender the whole field of such activity to the devil? Or, if we are not interested in making a decision about whether these things are "dynamite or delusion",[3] are we then simply to ignore the whole thing? Are we going to categorise these manifestations as irrelevant?

No sign has been more bitterly contested in our century than that which immediately marked the coming of the Spirit in Acts – the phenomenon of speaking in tongues. Glossalalia have been at the centre of an almost unbelievable saga of dispute. It has taken something like nine decades for the Church in the West to give any sort of general acceptance to this phenomenon. The rumbles are still being felt, of course, in many places. The change in attitude has not really been due to any new epoch-making theological exposition, but has rather been brought about by the massively increased weight of testimony. Tens of thousands of people today actually do speak in other tongues! Once people become aware of the widespread activity of the Spirit in the world, it is no longer possible for them to cry out that tongues are demonic abberations, as some Christians did in the aftermath of the Azusa Street outpouring in 1904. The godliness of the lives of so many of those who today speak in tongues and gain so much from it simply cannot be denied or ignored. In the same way, cries of "irrelevant!" or "for the less mature!" are accusations which no longer carry any weight, when it is only too obvious that there are many mature Christians who certainly do not find this particular sign irrelevant. The cry of "divisive!" has been sounded loudly and persistently. It has taken us a long time to acknowledge that it is not the sign itself which is divisive, but rather the reactions of Christian people to it. We have had to come to accept that a sign of the Spirit, whose very presence alone guarantees our unity and impels us towards it, cannot possibly be in itself divisive.

Yet, though better sense has finally begun to prevail, there remains an attitude which sometimes is all too ready to put the reality of such a gift on the shelf, rather than to move out positively to embrace it (and others like it) and taste its blessing. "Accept it if we must, but avoid it if we can — after all, there are more important things" becomes a kind of final line of defence. But the gift or sign of tongues continues to challenge us from the pages of Acts, and, having withstood all the blasts of dispensationalism, it still beckons us toward itself as a precious part of our inheritance in the Holy Spirit. It is not offered to us so that we might merely acknowledge and dissect it; rather, we are meant to reach out for it and enjoy it. If we do not enjoy it personally, we can at least enjoy it in the body of Christ.

I have not discussed the gift of tongues at such length because I think it is a more valuable indicator of a true coming of the Spirit than the other signs. I have considered it simply because it was such an early manifestation of sign and wonder in the Church of Acts, and because its history in the twentieth century offers one of the clearest examples of the reluctance with which the Church moves towards all that God can pour out in times of revival. The struggle over tongues indicates how much we can lose if we neglect and misread the divine blueprint.

From those initial supernatural manifestations the narrative in Acts moves swiftly along to the healing of the man at the Beautiful Gate of the Temple (Acts 2:1ff). This man was a cripple from birth, and whilst he was being carried to his lifelong begging place he was instantly healed in the Name of Jesus. Though Jesus had gone, first crucified and then resurrected and glorified, His Spirit was still abroad, and now one more person was added to the scores of those who had already received His healing touch. Other healings were to follow — many of them. Aeneas, a bedridden paralytic for eight years, began to walk (9:32);

Dorcas was raised from the dead (9:40); a man at Lystra, crippled from the day of his birth, "sprang up and walked" (14:10). The sick were carried into the streets and even Peter's shadow (and later Paul's handkerchiefs) became tools in the continuing healing ministry of Jesus. These are only some of the specific cases mentioned by Luke, and he is constantly reminding us that all the time "many signs and wonders were done by the apostles" – and others! Also Jesus' assault on the demonic kingdom, like His ministry of healing, was clearly continued by the Spirit through the disciples (Acts 8:7 etc.). Demon possession was real and was dealt with decisively.

Once again, in the face of such plainly stated activity, we are left a little mystified by the extraordinary furore that has surrounded the re-establishment of this dimension of the supernatural in the life of the Church (unless, of course, we recognise that the furore was essentially stirred up by those very powers who have most to lose!). Furore about healing there certainly has been, second only to that about tongues. It may well be that the inclusion of healing with tongues-speaking in the Pentecostal testimony of the first decades of this century resulted in a hardening of attitude towards this area of the supernatural. This hardness is only now beginning to soften in the Western world.

There really was no excuse for the long rejection of the dimension of healing. Testimonies of healing abounded well before the beginning of the twentieth century, and they were well authenticated. Some were quite extraordinary. W. H. Daniels, in his biography of Moody, relates the case of a worker who was recruited by Moody for his Gospel outreach in Chicago. He had a diseased leg which crippled him. The constant evangelistic visiting eventually left him in great pain. On the night just before going to see a doctor he asked the Lord to heal him. This was the testimony he was later to give: "I fell asleep and dreamed that I went to the surgeon . . . and that he cut open my leg, performed some operation which I did not comprehend, and immediately closed the wound again – not hurting me in the least or even leaving a scar." When he woke up the leg was perfectly healed — it was completely straight and was of the same length as his other leg. His work in evangelism continued with no disruption![4]

Why is it that such testimony is so often rejected? Whether we think that this dimension of Christian experience is not so important as preaching, or we feel uncomfortable swimming in what seem to be unpredictable and dangerous waters, or we are nervous about counterfeits, the fact of the matter is that God has continued to move in such ways. We must either recognise this or be prepared to consider as null and void a vast mountain of healing and deliverance!

Our God is a God who works in sign and wonder. Revival is a time when such workings are full and frequent. That much must be accepted, no matter how justified the calls for safeguards may be . If we are not open in spirit to God as He moves powerfully in such a manner, we are essentially not open to Him at all.

The purpose of sign and wonder

So we need not ask *whether* God moves in this sort of way; it is more edifying for us to ask *why* He does so. This is an important question. Jesus' own ministry was particularly stamped with sign and wonder, and His work through the Spirit in the early Church carried on the process. It can hardly be dubbed misguided or irrelevant. There must be very good reason for it and we have to be open to such ministry and to a restoration of it in the Church.

A number of reasons could be advanced. For instance, signs are called signs because they are powerful pictures of unseen spiritual truth and they have much to teach us. This is the primary emphasis in John's gospel. But when we come to look at the Acts blueprint, one feature seems to be pressed upon us more than any other, and that is that signs were the means by which God broke open whole cities and towns to hear the preaching of the Gospel. God could doubtless have done that without sign and wonder, but the fact is that

213

He chose to do it with them. At the very least we have to learn to allow God to do what He wants in the way He wants (even if He wants to work through sign and wonder!), and to examine such strategy. The biblical testimony is that sign and wonder are strategically tied to the preaching of the Gospel and the winning of many converts for Christ. They are striking instruments for providing an unparalleled platform for the communication of the Good News.

The impact which was made by the disciples on Jerusalem provides a remarkable example of this process. At the outset they were a mere one hundred and twenty strong. They were faced with the task of witnessing to a major city with a large population immensely swollen by the festivities of Pentecost. They had every conceivable disadvantage. The prospects for a "campaign" were very limited indeed. Yet the fact is that only a short time later, on the Day of Pentecost, Peter preached to multitudes. How did it happen? A phrase in Luke gives us the clue: "at this sound the multitude came together" (Acts 2:6). What "sound" does he refer to? There are two possibilities. First, it might have been the sound of the disciples speaking out in tongues, but that hardly seems credible. Secondly, it may well have been the sound of the "rushing, mighty wind". That great and powerful wind must have roared through at least a part of Jerusalem, and people must have heard it. It looks very much, therefore, as though they were drawn together by the roaring sound of the wind and then further amazed by the phenomenon of the disciples speaking in tongues. These two signs created a great platform for the preaching of the truth about Jesus. Peter wasted no time in explaining to the gathering crowds where the wind and the tongues had come from. It was an amazing opportunity to preach an exalted and resurrected Jesus, and with Holy Spirit boldness he seized it.

We can see the same process at work in the incident at the Beautiful Gate in which a cripple was healed (Acts 2:1ff). He kept close to Peter after his healing, and as he walked and leaped around the Temple precincts he was immediately recognised. The result was that "all the people ran together to them in Solomon's Portico in astonishment''. Again Peter launched into an explanation of what had happened, preaching an ascended Jesus who brought forgiveness of sin. Thus the Temple, the most strategic place in Jerusalem, became the centre of an extraordinary proclamation about the Jesus who had been recently condemned and crucified. The whole thing had been orchestrated, however, not by the disciples but by the Holy Spirit, who had drawn the crowds together through a divine healing.

The sequel is interesting. Such a happening obviously could not escape the notice of the religious hierarchy, and in the purpose of God it was not intended to. The apostles were imprisoned and the next morning were brought before the High Priest himself, the most significant members of his family and all the rulers, elders and scribes — the very highest company in the land! They demanded an explanation of the apostles. What they in fact heard from Peter's lips was the same Gospel as the crowds had heard. Moreover, the healed cripple himself stood alongside him as an unassailable witness to the truth of what he was preaching.

Similar platforms for the proclamation of the Gospel were created in many other places through signs and wonders. The whole of Lydda turned to the Lord when Aeneas was healed, and many believed in Joppa when Dorcas was healed. Lystra, Iconium, Ephesus and many more cities were opened wide to the preaching of the Gospel as they were stirred by sign and wonder.

It is no valid criticism of the powerful ability of sign and wonder to attract large crowds to say that among such crowds many would be attracted merely out of curiosity and even base intent. Of course, people like Simon Magus would be present and some of them, like him, might even get baptised, requiring a severe rebuke later on (Acts 8:13). Where large numbers gather, they will gather for all sorts of motives. Jesus was only too aware of this when He taught the five thousand (John 6). But many will gather out of genuine concern. As Jesus Himself reminds us, the net will gather all kinds of fish, but after the sorting process which follows, there will still be a good catch left. Our eyes must be fixed on that truth.

In the huge crowds that gathered around preachers like Tommy Hicks and George Jeffries there were plenty of people who laughed and mocked, and many who came just for excitement and to see the miracles. The same is true of the crowds which gather around Reinhard Bonnke today. But they are not essentially different from whose which followed Jesus. It was undoubtedly the case that the crowds to which Whitefield and Wesley preached were "motley" to a degree! We should not lightly dismiss or ignore the crowds which are gathering across the world in our own generation, nor should we dismiss the fact that frequently they gather in response to sign and wonder.

The context of sign and wonder

It is important at this point to draw attention to the fact that by the expression "sign and wonder" we do not simply mean the normal healing and deliverance ministries which may go on in the life of the Christian Church. The sign and wonder activity which we are witnessing in Acts is something which has a much wider dimension than that. It is intimately connected with the proclamation of the Gospel to unbelievers. Its context is the conversion of large numbers of people outside the Church. It is an expression of the power of the Spirit which impacts the community. The preaching of the Gospel, with subsequent conversions, is a paramount intention of God and the Spirit, and signs and wonders belong to that intention. The signs and wonders which Jesus performed during His ministry had a powerful impact. Undoubtedly there were moments when He ministered to His followers, but for the most part His miracle power was exercised among the ordinary run of people, and was designed specifically to challenge them.

If we think of sign and wonder as an activity which goes on only within the fellowship of a church, then no matter how valid that activity might be, we are really allowing it to drop below the place which it holds in Acts. If our vision for God to move with sign and wonder relates merely to the Church and does not entail a desire to see God's miracle-working power bringing the Gospel and salvation to unbelievers, then we are missing its most important aspect. The prayer of the Jerusalem church was twofold: "give us boldness to preach, while you stretch out your hand to heal and signs and wonders be done . . ." (Acts 4:29–30). Clearly, for them deeds of power were intimately connected with proclamation. Our attitude should be the same as theirs.

There are plenty of modern examples of sign and wonder occurring in this true context. A Chinese peasant woman had a growth the size of a basketball on the side of her body. She passed a building where fifty years before she had heard the Gospel. In agony and desperation she went into the building and was prayed for by the pastor. On her way home the growth subsided completely. A few days later she reappeared at the pastor's door with nine members of her family. Having seen what had happened to the old woman, they wanted to become Christians. A few weeks later fifteen carts arrived loaded with people and with charms, the latter to be burned the former to be converted. As the weeks went by literally hundreds found their way to that building and to Jesus.[5] This is biblical sign and wonder.

An Argentinian called Carlos Naranjo witnessed his wife being healed from an incurable disease through the Tommy Hicks' campaigns. He abandoned his former scepticism concerning healing and began preaching in a downtown area of St Nicholas. "Naranjo was mocked and stoned, but he preached under a tree in the middle of the slum. A breakthrough to the slum dwellers came when an infant was healed of a head deformity, the head bigger than the body. Many outstanding conversions followed, and the slum was transformed."[6]

What can be the possible objection to seeking God for such powerful and biblical activity, when the evidence shows that it gets through so forcefully to the poor and needy?

In all this we need to be quite clear in our minds that an

217

extraordinary manifestation of the supernatural, whether it be healing or something else, does not automatically lead people to put their faith in Jesus. Acts demonstrates this clearly. The fact that the man at the Beautiful Gate had been healed and that he stood personally before the elders of the Jews whilst Peter preached did not lead to any widespread conversion of the hierarchy. Their minds were far too set on their own religious views, and the jealousy that rose in their hearts towards the disciples effectively blocked a true spiritual reaction to the healing. They were not averse, perhaps, to a healing, provided it was done decently. But they were unwilling to accept a healing which was associated with the vulgarity of crowds and unlearned fishermen!

People are converted to Christ by preaching and conviction, not by sign and wonder. This is a clear fact. However, I think it is important to note that the manifestation of sign and wonder is not simply something that creates a platform for preaching. Rather, it actually becomes a vehicle for conviction to spread through a crowd of people. When God moves in power through supernatural manifestation there is frequently released a sense of deep astonishment and awe. It may not happen to all, but it will happen to some. There will be occasions when it will in fact be felt by the vast majority.

Acts gives us a very clear insight into this connection between conviction and sign and wonder. In the very first reference to the apostles doing such powerful deeds we see a close link between those deeds and the creation of a sense of awe (Acts 2:43). Precisely the same link is seen later in Acts 5:12–13, where we are told that there was such a sense of the power associated with the apostles that "none of the rest dared join them". This incident followed on very closely from the episode in which two simple declarations made by Peter over Ananias and Sapphira had resulted in both of them falling dead under the judgement of God. Thought quite the opposite to the normal sign of healing, this particular sign brought a tremendous fear of God upon the local community.

When God is working powerfully in supernatural manifestation the sense of awe is not likely to be far away, for we are witnessing a revelation of His presence. So the cultured Sergius Paulus, "a man of intelligence", was stunned by the manner in which Paul called down blindness on the magician at Paphos, and consequently believed (Acts 13:12).

Moving on with wonders

Of course, we should not be gullible about sign and wonder, and we should test the source of such activity. There is one very obvious test which, if observed, would clear a great deal of the doubt and misunderstanding that still surrounds the subject. The test is simply this: counterfeit sign and wonder is hardly likely to coexist with clear preaching of salvation through the blood and sacrifice of the Son of God. Wherever the name of Jesus is exalted as incarnate Lord and people are called to give heart and life to Him in order to pursue a life of righteousness through His Spirit, any accompanying supernatural works are not likely to have a satanic origin. How much heartbreak would have been avoided in early Pentecostal days if those who opposed the new-style evangelists had only carefully considered the Gospel which they were preaching. It was clearly of God, as indeed were the signs.

This is not to say that even among Christians the flesh cannot obtrude on the spiritual. Of course it can − and in the area of the supernatural we have a platform for exhibitionists and attention-seekers, and also easy ground for foolish obsessions amongst those who are immature. That constitutes a call for pastoral care. More dangerous are the pseudo-Christians who frequently associate with sign and wonder ministries, but whose lives betray nothing of the fruit of righteousness that marks out the true Christian. We have to remember there were quite a few such pseudo-Christians in the New Testament Church. Today we have the same need as they had then − a need for discernment.

219

We need to be firm against the spurious, and equally to be strong to encourage genuine works of power.

In thinking of revival, therefore, we are thinking essentially of sign and wonder as the consort of strong, powerful Gospel preaching and witness. Simply because of the extraordinary way in which sign and wonder have frequently been part of the Holy Spirit's strategy to accelerate the growth of the Church and to make a powerful impact on the world of unbelievers, we cannot afford to ignore them. On the contrary, despite the problems they may bring, sign and wonder are things to be sought after, more especially in a society that is getting more multicultural and possibly more open and responsive to such manifestations. We must take our stand where the Christians in the early Church took their stand and cry out with them: "Stretch out your hand to heal and perform miraculous signs and wonders!"

Notes

1. Ross Paterson, *Heart Cry For China*, p. 196.
2. Alison Griffiths, *Fire in the Islands*, p. 175.
3. *Dynamite or Delusion* is the title of a recent publication by Gervase Angel.
4. W. H. Daniels, *D. L. Moody*, pp. 84-86.
5. Ross Paterson, op. cit., p. 164.
6. Edwin Orr, *Evangelical Awakenings in Latin America*, p. 191.

Chapter 13: Evangelists and Evangelism

Philip went down to a city of Samaria and preached to them Christ.

Acts 8:5

There were some, men of Cyprus and Cyrene, who, on coming to Antioch, spoke to the Greeks also, preaching the Lord Jesus.

Acts 11:20

It would be a gross mistake to think that the blueprint of revival which is provided for us by the Book of Acts ends with the account of the extraordinary happenings in Jerusalem. Acts is a continuous history and spans some three decades, starting with the ascension of Jesus in AD 29 and concluding with Paul's imprisonment in AD 60. Its contents embrace the progress of the Gospel from Jerusalem and Palestine through to the north-eastern area of the Mediterranean and ultimately to Rome itself. The blueprint of revival comprises all this.

It is important for us to grasp this clearly. We not only need to examine the extraordinary happenings of the Day of Pentecost and of its immediate aftermath, but we also need to appreciate the long-term impact of the outpouring of the Holy Spirit. We should not simply close our eyes after the early years, but we should instead seek the longer perspective.

Perhaps one of the clearest and most obvious features of Luke's account is the fact that the outpouring of the Spirit on the Day of Pentecost produced a blaze of evangelism that lasted throughout those three decades and even beyond.

Quite rightly, many have pointed out that revival is something which takes us beyond the realm of evangelism. Evangelism is not revival. There is a depth and a width in the manifestation of the presence of God in revival which is quite different from evangelism as ordinarily experienced. That is very true, but the pattern of Acts reveals absolutely without question that when there is a revival move of the Holy Spirit, evangelism is a most significant (perhaps *the* most significant) aspect of the "fall-out". There cannot be a true and full outpouring of the Holy Spirit which does not usher in powerful evangelism. If this aspect is missing, whatever else the Spirit may be doing, we are lacking a fulfilment of the complete pattern of revival, and we must press on until it is with us.

Our expectation of powerful movements of evangelism as an integral part of revival is based on the very nature of the promise of the Spirit with which Acts starts. "You will receive power when the Holy Spirit comes upon you, and you will be my witnesses" were the words which Jesus spoke. From the very start, therefore, the promise was intimately bound up with witnessing. Jesus wanted to make this very clear to His disciples, since their thinking was actually going in the opposite direction. It was Israel they had in mind, not the world! "Is this the time for restoring the kingdom to Israel?" was their question. "No, this is the time for world-wide witness!" was the essence of Jesus' response (Acts 1: 6−8). Our own hearts can so easily follow the thinking of the disciples and, like them, reckon that the coming of the Spirit is designed to centre simply on the Church as it now is. We need to understand clearly that the Holy Spirit is a supreme Witness (Acts 5:32), and that when He comes in all His power witnessing becomes inescapable − indeed, predominant!

The evangelists of the early Church

The Book of Acts reveals that the outpouring of the Spirit had a major effect on evangelism in two essential directions. First, it depicts the emergence of some very powerful individual evangelists, through whom the Gospel was preached with extraordinary results. Secondly, it constantly makes reference to believers who actively spoke about Christ wherever they went. In this way it presents a balanced picture of the Body of Christ. It was full of the Spirit, making a great impact on the world both through individual preachers and through believers in general.

The band of apostolic preachers which was unleashed on the Day of Pentecost very quickly produced a harvest of highly gifted people. We shall never know all of them, but Luke selects two of them — Stephen and Philip — for special attention. These men became believers probably within a few weeks of Pentecost, and not long after they began to preach with great power among the unconverted. They were men who were "born in the fire" and they inevitably "carried the fire". This is one of the great hallmarks of revival. It tends to produce great evangelists who then, in turn, stimulate further revivals.

Stephen's career was all too short. He quickly met martyrdom. But it was a career of great importance. Full of faith and full of the Spirit, he preached with a wisdom and an understanding of the Scriptures that overwhelmed his hearers in the Hellenist synagogues. "The word of God was increasing and the disciples were multiplying greatly" (Acts 6:7). He was a man who was almost too far ahead in his understanding. He knew, and was not afraid to say, that the day of the Temple and the Law had to give way to the day of the Christ. Not many, perhaps, saw this as clearly as Stephen, and he paid for his forthright understanding with his life. But he left a fire burning into the old order. Moreover, he left a fire burning into the conscience of Saul of Tarsus, who was chief witness to his martyrdom. When he died the fire he had kindled was not extinguished. Rather, the flame grew stronger.

Philip was a man of similar calibre. Like Stephen, he fearlessly preached Christ. After his friend's martyrdom he went down to the chief city in Samaria, and with great breadth of vision and boldness of heart preached Christ to the hated Samaritans. He might well have trembled — behind him were Jews bent on persecution and in front of him were the traditionally hostile Samaritans. But God used him powerfully, and multitudes responded to his preaching. There were many baptisms and much joy. A whole new field of opportunity was open.

With a deft stroke Luke then shows us this same man being swiftly removed from the crowds and engaging in powerful personal work. He gives us a fullish account of how a high-ranking Ethiopian was led to Christ by Philip on a desert road. We are left meditating on the powerful way in which the Spirit can work strategically through an evangelist who can hear His voice — for through that one convert no doubt the whole of Ethiopia was given a witness for Christ.

What price can be placed on such men in the ongoing life of the Church? They are amongst the greatest gifts which the Church can ever receive: they are Christ's gifts. It is so important that we see clearly that when we are seeking God for revival we are seeking for a move of the Spirit in which this sort of evangelist emerges from the midst of the Church. The outpouring of the Spirit in revival is the very stream from which the most powerful evangelism flows. That is why revival is so important.

Perhaps one point in particular could be underlined here, and that is the length of Philip's ministry. Stephen, as we have seen, enjoyed only a very short ministry. Philip, however, fared quite differently. Acts shows us that some twenty-five years later he was giving hospitality to Paul at the end of Paul's third missionary tour. His daughters (all prophets) were also with him. This is a pointer to and an illustration of something of the greatest importance, namely that the ministries which are set up in times of revival can and do frequently go on for a long time. Philip is referred to explicitly at this point as "Philip the evangelist". We do not know what he did between the conversion of the Ethiopian and the meeting with Paul, but we may be sure he exercised a ministry in which the early fire continued to burn. Therefore the evangelistic ministries which are the consequence of visitations of the Spirit can be both deep and long-lasting, and this is one of the great glories of such visitations.

It would be absurd to say that it takes a revival to produce evangelists for the Church. They are always there, as are the teachers and the pastors, but times of revival both swell their number and give their ministries a very significantly deeper spiritual note.

It would seem to me that frequently the Church in times of dryness loses not only its evangelistic fervour but also its awareness of the evangelist as a gift to the Body of Christ. There are also times when churches may be aware, at least doctrinally, of the need for evangelism, but become somewhat unbalanced and think that the local church membership is the only vehicle of evangelism. This is as much a mistake as relying exclusively on an evangelist. The evangelist is a very clear and biblically recognised gift to the Church of God. His is a ministry of the utmost importance and consequence for the work of extending the Church and reaping spiritual harvests amongst unbelievers. Revival has a habit of restoring this precious gift to the life of the Church, and it is one of the continuing effects of revival, even when the initial flames have died somewhat.

Revival evangelists – gifts from God

This fact is worth dwelling on for a moment. To find an illustration of it we do not need to move out of our own century. I think it may be a challenge yet to the traditions of some if I take the example of two young brothers who were converted during the Welsh Revival of 1904, and whose ministries perhaps still need a fuller recognition.

These two young men were Stephen and George Jeffreys. Stephen had worked in the mines since the age of twelve and he was twenty-eight when he was "gloriously converted and immediately filled with indescribable joy" at the Siloh Chapel in the village of Nantyffillon. George was a little younger. His biographer tells us that "in that divinely charged atmosphere, Stephen started preaching on the streets of Maesteg — for several years he continued working as a coal-miner but at every opportunity he preached in the open air. Prayer meetings were the order of the day and Stephen was faithful also in that."[1]

Two years later (1908) they both felt the impact of the Pentecostal outpouring in Alexander Boddy's church in Sunderland as its influence reached Wales. At special meetings at Maesteg the brothers received "a mighty baptism of the Holy Spirit".

Stephen Jeffreys' first invitation to conduct an evangelistic campaign came in 1913. George joined him. It was an extraordinary campaign. A magistrate writing in the *Life of Faith* said that the fervour of the meetings was as great as that seen in 1904. There were many conversions and some remarkable cases of healing, and the presence of God was very evident "day after day and night after night".

That was the start of two outstanding ministries of evangelism which had a very powerful impact in Britain (and beyond). Stephen died in 1943 and George in 1962. For a whole generation they moved up and down the country, filling the largest halls to overflowing and ministering with immense power and consequence. This description of the scenes at Stephen's great East London campaigns in 1925 is typical of the reports about his ministry:

Each week the crowds have grown in numbers, and the interest in the mission has become more intense, till in the closing stages hundreds of people have, in the interests of public safety, had to be denied admission . . . The pastor appears to have drawn the people to the meeting by some magnetic power, and, as if caught in the wave of a great religious revival, hundreds have stood in the assemblies and professed conversion . . . Great meetings have been held in the afternoons and evenings throughout the week, and the scenes witnessed have been absolutely without parallel in the life of the town.[2]

As for George's meetings, the comments were very similar. In Birmingham in 1930, for example, the huge Bingley Hall was the scene of twenty-six meetings. The hall was packed out on each occasion and conversions and healings were thick and fast. There had been nothing like this before except the campaigns of Moody in 1875 and those of Torrey in 1904. It was a similar story in all the other main cities of Britain. In London between 1926 and 1939 the Albert Hall was filled fifty times and the Crystal Palace seven times. Always there were conversions, baptisms and healings.

The upshot of it all was the emergence of the Elim and Assemblies of God churches — two powerful and vigorous spiritual movements, each boasting many thousands of followers. Perhaps the significance of this activity of God between the two world wars has yet to be fully recognised. But at the very least we are discussing here the unleashing of two very remarkable men, both products of revival, into a brand of evangelism that had an impact throughout the whole country and bore fruit which still persists.

We could go to the other side of the globe and find a similar phenomenon taking place in China. At the turn of the century two elderly ladies, responding to a plea from a missionary, began to pray for revival in the district of Hinghwa. It broke out during the Easter of 1909, when the Cross was preached. "A purified church became a witnessing church and within a month or two there were 3,000 conversions." Amongst those 3,000 was a nine-year-old boy, John Sung. He found Christ with bitter tears of repentance.

His life was soon marked by an exceptional love for the Word of God, an unusual desire to pray and a passion to preach. John was the son of a pastor, and at the age of fourteen began to deputise for his father when he was away. His preaching was vivid and much appreciated.

He had a brilliant academic career in America, only to turn his back on it and pursue a totally dedicated evangelistic, even apostolic, ministry. He became known, not without warrant, as the Wesley of China. For some sixteen years, until he died in 1944 at the age of forty-three, he blazed a trail through China and adjacent countries in a manner which radically enlivened Christians and brought thousands to Christ.

The following, written by Leslie Lyle, is typical of the reports of his ministry: "When Sung came to Sibu [Sarawak] in 1936, in ten days 1,600 Chinese found their way to Christ and more than a 100 offered themselves for active service in God's kingdom.[3] In that same year during a week-long campaign at Surabaja 5,000 people streamed in daily to hear the evangelist speak. Thousands would take their place at 8 a.m. in order to obtain a seat, and would remain there until 11 p.m. at night when the last of the three or four meetings finally ended."[4] Kurt Koch remarks: "I have never known in my experience such a campaign . . . where people have endured some 10 to 15 hours of preaching the Word of God each day for 10 solid days on end."

When Lyle looked for evidence of lasting fruit from Sung's ministry some ten years after his death, he found it on every hand. A tour of South-East Asia revealed Sung converts everywhere. They were very frequently men and women in the most responsible positions in the churches, and their witness had the fiery stamp of the one who had brought them to Christ. Commenting on Sung's ministry, Lyle writes: "Singapore, the tiny island state with over a million Chinese living there, will never forget the man whose ministry exploded upon the churches with such power." He also remarks: "In Indonesia one could not escape from the universal influence of Dr Sung, whose two evangelistic journeys in 1939 stirred the entire Chinese community."[5]

Let us turn to the career of Billy Graham for a final illustration. Edwin Orr records that in 1941 a Lutheran pastor in Los Angeles began a ministry of encouraging other pastors to pray for genuine revival. In 1949 some 300 ministers were still praying and attending a half-night of prayer. There followed a series of revivals in Christian colleges throughout North America. In particular an extraordinary revival movement occurred at a conference

228

for college students in California. It was there that Billy Graham received an immediate call to his world-wide ministry. Out of that revival came also the ministry of William Bright, the founder of Campus Crusade. Orr comments: "The outstanding development of the mid-century revival was the emergence of Billy Graham as a world evangelist in the tradition of Whitefield, Finney and Moody. His great campaigns of evangelism broke all records in reaching a vast number of human beings."[6]

The catalogue of the men and women who have been the evangelistic firebrands ignited by revival is a very long one, and one that needs to be viewed carefully by any who doubt the long-term efficacy of powerful outpourings of the Spirit. We might add also that those who have caught the fire of genuine revival have always taken something of its flame with them. It is not fashionable now to call evangelistic campaigns "revival meetings", but one can certainly understand why they were at one time given that name. The sort of evangelistic campaigns which the Jeffreys brothers or John Sung or Wesley or Charles Finney held had without any shadow of doubt a true aroma of revival-burning about them. Indeed, when we are talking about the eighteenth-century revival which was led by the Wesleys and Whitefield, we are in fact essentially talking about a national (even international) evangelistic campaign lasting for several decades. The campaign can be justly called a revival because of the numbers converted, the weight of the conviction experienced and the extent of the work done. It was the same with John Sung, for as Kurt Koch points out, "wherever he went there was a spiritual revival: men acknowledged their sins, enemies were reconciled, stolen goods were returned".

Revival is above all else a deep work done in the heart: it is a perception of Jesus, of His work at Calvary and of the glory of His salvation so clear and strong as to cause a burning of faith and devotion. It is really here that the secret of revival evangelists is to be found. For evangelism should not primarily be seen as methods of witness applied with clinical, orthodox precision. Such evangelism is always

229

honoured by God, for God loves all evangelism, but it is not to be compared with that which flows out of a heart burning with love of Jesus. This is what is required, and it is this which times of revival provide.

That is why we are not surprised, therefore, to read of Stephen Jeffreys that "a flame was kindled in his heart at conversion which could never be extinguished. Calvary wasn't just an event in history — it was a mighty power which burned at the very centre of his being,"[7] or to read that "he loved to see souls making their way to the Cross. He literally gloried in the all-conquering power of the Gospel to save to the uttermost."[8] John Sung very nearly lost his vital faith in Jesus through the modernism that closed in on him at an American seminary, but when God restored it to him during a spell in a mental hospital it was of a kind that caused his ministry to burst into flame. With great vividness he saw that his role was to be a John the Baptist, and nothing could stop him in his powerful demands for purity and repentance. Towards the end of his relatively short life his friends pressed him to seek medical advice, but his only reply was, "I haven't the time. I must preach the Gospel."

Evangelistic fire in the Church at large

When we think of revival we tend to think of the great individuals like Stephen and Philip in Acts, and the Jeffreys brothers and Sung and Wesley in more recent history, but we need to be aware also that when the Spirit is truly at work in power, large numbers of unrecorded witnesses and evangelists surround them. So in Acts, before we read of Philip's great campaign in Samaria, we read that those who were scattered by the persecution went everywhere, preaching the Gospel. Revival is very much a precise fulfilment of the words, "The Lord gave the word: great was the company of those who preached it."

Donald Gee, the Pentecostal statesman and author, made these remarks about Stephen Jeffrey's ministry:

One significant and fruitful result of [that] memorable ministry . . . was the way it inspired so many other men to attempt big things for God. A veritable wave of evangelism and evangelists followed in his train. Some of these efforts were all too obviously an attempt to imitate the style and method of Stephen Jeffreys without his unique spiritual gifts and personality: but for all that the aggregate results were impressive. New assemblies were being opened continuously, and a new urge to public testimony of a bolder order swept like fresh air through little faithful groups of believers who for years had seemed content to lie hidden in odd corners and back streets.[9]

A powerful evangelistic impetus given by one man, whom the Spirit of God is using mightily, very quickly generates the same impetus in the lives of many others. Powerful evangelism always creates evangelists as well as converts. The passing of the fire from one coal to another is wonderful to watch! All true revivals have seen something of this.

One of the most attractive examples of this is to be found in that move of the Holy Spirit in which Primitive Methodism was born. This happened at the very start of the nineteenth century, when God raised up Hugh Bourne and William Clowes. The writer J. Ritson has described them as possessing a "primitive fire" of a "singularly ardent and explosive type".[10] Through their work and influence hundreds of utterly morally decadent villages throughout Britain were greatly moved by the Gospel for well over half a century. They shared a "passionate zeal for the salvation of their fellows".[11] They "made ceaseless war upon the kingdom of darkness" and brought salvation to thousands.

These men certainly did not do all the work themselves. Their influence was felt most through a number of extraordinary preachers who caught the fire with which their great leaders burned. Few people may have heard of John Wedgwood, John Benton, Johnny Oxtoby, Thomas Batty and Joseph Spoor, but these men were nothing less than tigers for God. Ritson writes:

231

their Herculean labours, their hairbreadth escapes, their quenchless zeal, their dauntless courage, their unfailing audacity, their fierce fight with poverty and hunger and weariness and mob brutality, and the marvellous and permanent success they achieved is one long romance which has added a new and brilliant chapter to the Acts of the Apostles.[12]

These are no empty words, as the records of their lives show. Dressed in homespun, living on the most meagre of food, they were great men of prayer. For example, Oxtoby regularly spent six hours a day in prayer and walked huge distances to preach. Despite having very little schooling, they spoke with amazing fluency and power. Together they built up whole circuits of new churches. Moreover, among them were numbered some women preachers of rare power. A certain Elizabeth Bultitude, for example, "travelled thousands on thousands of miles, often preaching five and six times a week, three and some five times on the Sabbath, and frequently visiting and praying with from ten to forty families a day".[13] The records show that there was "a host of women preachers . . . who married ministers and continued, as occasion offered, to preach the Gospel".[14]

These were the true heirs of Wesley's field army of evangelists and lay preachers. They were great gifts to the Church of God and to a needy society. Such people are among the most powerful expressions of revival activity.

Returning for a moment to John Sung, we should note he was not simply a mighty evangelist but was also the instigator of evangelism on a wide front, carried out by hundreds of his committed converts. His ministry provides a startling example of a process which is frequently seen in revival. Very quickly, the revival fire is taken up by teams of newly converted people and spread to other parts. After one of Sung's ten-day missions, for example, 116 teams were formed to go out into the villages surrounding the town in which the campaign had been held. They were just three-person teams, but they were powerful. Kurt Koch comments:

"The work of the teams, who constantly maintained their witness despite later occupation by the Japanese, is significant. Their work never faltered even amidst the confusion of war."[15] Whether in China or Argentina or Seoul, wherever there has been an outbreak of revival fire there has always been a spontaneous and powerful spreading of the fire by very significant numbers of people, and the leadership of the churches has given it the greatest priority.

Of course, the same Spirit gave definite and outstanding gifts of evangelism to certain individuals who also gave rank-and-file church members the desire to share the Gospel. In Acts we are shown clearly that as a consequence of Stephen's martyrdom and the persecution which followed, *"those who were scattered, went about preaching the word"* (Acts 8:4). Undoubtedly they received a great stimulus from those who had a distinct call of evangelism on their lives, such as Philip, but they may well have been in their turn a great stimulus to those evangelists. It is all the coals together in the fire, large and small, that allow the continued generation of heat and fire!

This, then, is the ongoing feature of revival: anointed and heartfelt evangelistic preaching by men raised up for the task. There are many towering figures among them, but there are very many more figures who are smaller and yet greatly effective. They spring up from the activity of the Spirit, who moves in the Church and gives a general longing and readiness to witness to its members.

When we seek revival we seek this liberating dynamic which gives an impetus to evangelism that no amount of training or planning can provide. We must pray for the Church to be constantly recharged with this dynamic.

Notes

1. Colin Whittaker, *Seven Pentecostal Pioneers*, p. 49.
2. E. Jeffreys, *Stephen Jeffreys*, pp. 54–56.
3. K. Koch, *The Revival in Indonesia*, p. 54.
4. L. Lyle, *John Sung* (Preface to fourth edition).

5. K. Koch, op. cit., p. 42.
6. Edwin Orr, *Evangelical Awakenings in Latin America*, p. 118.
7. E. Jeffreys, op. cit., p. 4.
8. Ibid., p. 65, quoting Pastor E. C. Boulton.
9. Ibid., p. 82, quoting Donald Gee.
10. J. Ritson, *The Romance of Primitive Methodism*, p. 55.
11. Ibid., p. 55.
12. Ibid., p. 99.
13. Ibid., p. 152.
14. Ibid., p. 153.
15. K. Koch, op. cit., p. 55.

Every revival in the homelands is felt within a decade on the foreign mission fields.

J. Edwin Orr

Baptise the nations; far and nigh
The triumphs of the Cross record:
The name of Jesus glorify,
Till every kindred call him Lord!

Moravian missionary hymn

Flow, river, flow;
Flood the nations with grace and glory.
Send forth your word, Lord;
And let there be light.

Graham Kendrick

Chapter 14: Cross-Cultural Mission

When the Holy Spirit come on you ... you shall be witnesses to the ... ends of the earth.

Acts 1:8

Revival and missionary vision

The Acts of the Apostles is not only a great revival document ... it is also a great missionary document. It starts in Jerusalem with the commission to witness in all the world which Jesus gives to the disciples, and it ends in Rome after surveying the advance of the Gospel through a most strategic part of the Roman Empire. Its pages show us Peter, Paul, Barnabas, Silas and many others evangelising the great pagan cities of the Mediterranean world, and thus provide us with an abundance of material for the study of missionary principles and strategy.

Acts not only describes the penetration of many different geographical areas, but it also describes how a small group of Jewish Christians broke through the great Jewish-Gentile divide and made possible the development of thoroughly indigenous Gentile churches. We are given, in other words, a clear picture of cross-cultural mission in action. We find ourselves witnessing a scene in which men and women of many races and cultures are called to acknowledge Jesus as Lord and to receive salvation by faith in Him alone.

From the very beginnings of the Christian Church, therefore, revival and missionary activity have gone hand in hand. Orr's comment that "every revival of religion in the homelands is felt on the foreign mission fields within a decade" is abundantly vindicated by the narrative in Acts. It took less than five years for the Gospel to reach both the

Samaritans and the Gentiles, and in less than thirty years large Gentile congregations were to be found all over Asia Minor and parts of Europe.

The reason why revival and mission are so closely bound together is to be found in the very terms of the promise which Jesus made to His disciples about the coming of the Spirit. Though the promise spoke first of a dynamic — "you shall have power" — it also spoke about a direction — "you shall be witnesses in all the world". Both dynamic and direction were indissolubly linked. The promised Spirit came to provide not just empowering, but empowering for nothing less than total world mission. Therefore the full outworking of the revival promise inevitably found expression in powerful and penetrating missionary expansion. Mission had to come out of Pentecost, because mission was essentially a part of Pentecost.

This means that wherever the Holy Spirit is poured out in full measure, there is sure to be a resurgence not only of spiritual power but also of vision for the spread of the Kingdom world-wide. The Spirit will come not only to empower His people but also to enlarge their hearts, so that they will have a passion for world mission. This is why revival is so important for mission. Revival re-establishes a sense of world-wide direction and motivation wherever that has been lacking in the Church. An unclouded sense of direction allied to a clear apprehension of the dynamic is the true starting-point of effective missionary activity. Revival is God's way of getting the Church mobilised for the task of mission. That is why missionary thinking must never stray from contemplating and seeking revival.

If, then, we want to discover the full meaning of the Pentecostal promise in order to pray for revival, we must embrace the direction as well as the dynamic. We must set ourselves to become world-orientated. If we are lacking this orientation, then we do not yet have the full measure of the revival vision. We must not let our concept of revival shrink to any less a canvas than the world scene.

The significance of tongues

Not only are revival and mission linked in the initial promise of the Spirit, but they are also linked by one of the first manifestations of the Spirit on the Day of Pentecost. When the Spirit came He supernaturally caused the disciples to pour out their hearts to God in languages representative of many different parts of the world. This was of great significance. The gift of tongues may well have been a sign that the Spirit had come, but it was more specifically a sign of something else. It was a sign that in the purposes of God the time had now come for the Gentiles to be brought into the Kingdom so that they might glorify Him across the world. What more appropriate sign of His intentions could God have given than to cause the disciples to break out in Gentile tongues? What clearer pointer could He have given to the task that lay ahead of the Church?

Unfortunately, in the modern debate on tongues we have altogether lost sight of the fundamental fact that before all else this gift was a sign. Of course it was a gift which many would have found helpful devotionally; of course it was a sign of the Spirit coming in power. But these things were not its essential function. Its real purpose was to point to world-wide conversions. The very fact that it came on the day when the Jews celebrated the firstfruits of the harvest reinforced the message that it was fruit from the Gentile world that God was seeking. As long as the gift of tongues remains a part of the outpourings of the Spirit, it links those outpourings with world mission. It is a sign.

Incidentally, when we perceive the real nature of the gift of tongues we understand why it has never been removed from the Church. We are still in the age of witnessing to the ends of the earth — we still live under the sign. There is absolutely no reason why it should not be a recurring sign throughout the Christian era. Indeed, one might say that as the movement towards greater and greater harvest across the world gathers momentum, we should all the more expect a manifestation of the sign. Perhaps that is why the gift of tongues has become so much more evident in our own times than in any other period of Church history. It is something we should look at not with disdain or mistrust but with great joy and thankfulness. It is a sign which no doubt Satan hates, for it speaks of a harvest for Jesus and a plundering of some of Satan's long-held strongholds.

The Great Awakening and missions

The perception of the world-wide proclamation of the Gospel as a part of the full revival vision has always been present amongst those who have most strenuously worked for revival. There is no clearer illustration of this than that found in the outlook of Jonathan Edwards and some of his contemporaries. Their vision and prayer were revival-centred, and their concern for the world did much to bring the great modern missionary movement into being.

As we saw earlier in this book, Edwards was much involved in the Great Awakening in the American colonies at the beginning of the eighteenth century. At that time the extent of evangelical Christian witness in the world was very limited indeed. For all intents and purposes it was to be found only in parts of Europe and on the eastern seaboard of North America. The great continents of Africa, Asia and South America were virtually untouched. Moreover, there was very little vision for reaching those areas, and even less activity. It was the sort of age in which the world-wide directive of Jesus was unlikely to flourish in any but the most perceptive of hearts. Yet we find in the midst of this dampening atmosphere a group of men ardent in their vision for revival and simultaneously ardent in their vision for the world-wide extension of the Gospel. Jonathan Edwards was a leading figure among them.

His experiences of revival in New England in the 1730s made a great impact on him. His written accounts of them resulted in his having some very significant correspondence with a number of leading Scottish ministers. In 1744, prompted by this correspondence, those Scottish ministers formed a prayer union for "intercession on behalf of the world-wide extension and prosperity of the Kingdom of Christ". They saw revivals and the winning of "the heathen" as being very closely linked. They agreed that a part of each Saturday evening and each Sunday morning as well as four specific days in the year should be given over to what was described as "united, extraordinary supplications to the God of all grace . . . that he would manifest his compassion to the world of mankind, by an abundant effusion of his Spirit on all the churches and the whole habitable earth". Here was a remarkable expression of the exact intent of Jesus' promise to the disciples about the coming of the Spirit. "Effusion of the Spirit" and "the whole habitable earth" were phrases which spoke clearly of the dynamic and directive contained in that promise. To these men it seemed obvious that the Gospel must go into all the earth and that the way in which it would do so successfully would be through successive and powerful outpourings of the Holy Spirit.

Notice of the formation of this prayer union was passed on to people whose vision was international. Wesley was informed, and so was Jonathan Edwards. Edwards' response, like Wesley's, was immediate and positive. He wrote back to Scotland: "Such an agreement and practice appears to me exceedingly beautiful, and becoming Christians." Thereafter he kept the vision constantly in front of his congregation.

In 1746 the prayer union, which was called the Concert for United Prayer, was extended by its Scottish promoters for another seven years, and the venture was strengthened by the publication of a "Memorial" outlining its intentions. Edwards immediately added his own contribution to this literature by publishing in 1747 a treatise with a very long but very significant title: *An Humble Attempt to Promote Explicit Agreement and Visible Union of God's People in Extraordinary Prayer, for the Revival of Religion and the Advancement of Christ's Kingdom on Earth, pursuant to Scripture-Promises and Prophecies concerning the Last*

Time. In this remarkable call to united prayer, Edwards set out his firm faith in the eventual overthrow of unbelief in Christendom, the conversion of the Jews and the enlightenment of all "Mohamedan" and "heathen" nations. In his book *The Puritan Hope*, Iain Murray wrote: "Edwards believed beforehand in the great missionary advance and saw, by faith, the gospel of Christ throughout all parts of Africa, Asia, America and Terra Australis." Like his Scottish brethren, he did not expect it to happen all at once, but rather as the result of successive revivals which would occur in answer to prayer.

Two fascinating episodes in Edwards' career seem to have put the seal of God on his vision. The first was the final phase of his ministry, in which he spent his time preaching to the native Indians at Stockbridge in New England. In this way he actually became part of the vision for which he was calling people to pray. The other and perhaps more important episode was his involvement with David Brainerd, who was already a missionary to the Indians and working not far from Edwards. It was through Brainerd's utterly dedicated ministry that in 1745 a revival broke out among the Indians in which great numbers of them were thoroughly converted. Edwards quickly became aware of this, and it gave him very real evidence of what revival could do among "the heathen". Clearly what God had done among the Indians was but a miniscule of what He could do in all the world. Furthermore, Brainerd eventually left what remained of his personal diary to Edwards. Edwards felt strongly that he should publish it, and thus the diary became in effect the first full-scale missionary biography ever to be produced. Its influence for stimulating prayer and missionary work was immense, and that influence is still with us, of course, even today. The personal link between these two men was a tremendous example of the relationship between revival (represented by Edwards) and mission (represented by Brainerd). It pointed prophetically to the outpourings of the Spirit that were to take place on mission fields in later years.

Nineteenth-century revivals and missions

The work of Jonathan Edwards was very influential not only in the earlier part of the eighteenth century but also in its crucial later decades, during which the modern world-wide missionary movement gradually got under way. One of the key figures in that movement was William Carey, and he was profoundly influenced by Edwards. In 1792 Carey, along with a handful of friends, formed the Baptist Missionary Society, and a year later he sailed for India. His personal example and the organisation which he founded were immensely influential and set the scene for the rapid development of the denominational missionary societies, which were to open missions in many different parts of the world in the early 1800s.

William Carey's bold step only came, however, as a result of nearly a decade of earnest prayer for "the general revival and spread of religion". The group which engaged in this visionary praying and sent Carey on his way owed their inspiration in large measure to Edwards' writings, not least to his *Humble Attempt to Promote Extraordinary Prayer*. So important was this kind of prayer to them that they had themselves reissued the *Humble Attempt* in order to encourage others to engage in it. Needless to say, a copy went with Carey to India. He wanted to recruit missionaries who would treat prayer as a top priority. He wrote, "above all, missionaries must be instant in prayer for the effusion of the Holy Spirit upon the people in their charge".

The prayer group from which Carey's initiative developed was not a solitary phenomenon — rather, such groups became widespread. Orr writes: "William Carey . . . was one of a group who first set up in England the simultaneous prayer union that spread throughout evangelical Christendom and achieved its avowed purpose in the revival of religion and the extension of the kingdom of God overseas." Noting the extension of such praying to America, Orr tells us: "Isaac Backus and his friends in New England

243

adopted the British Plan for a general Concert of Prayer for the revival of religion and extension of religion abroad. Prayer meetings multiplied as church members devoted the first Monday of every month to fervent intercession." The "British Plan" he refers to involved evangelical ministers in all denominations, including the Church of England and the Church of Scotland. Orr sums up the influence of this movement thus: "the concert of prayer remained the significant factor in the recurring revivals of religion and the extraordinary out-thrust of missions for a full fifty years".

This link between prayer for revival and world-wide mission was never lost throughout the whole of the nineteenth century. The great mid-century revivals in America and Britain tremendously strengthened the denominational missions that had begun to form in Carey's time. Moreover, the same revivals provided the inspiration for a very powerful new instrument for world mission – the interdenominational society. This was to set the pace for mission in the last decades of the century, just as the denominational society had done in the earlier decades.

The final decade of the nineteenth century, like the final decade of the previous century, ended on a very high note of prayer and expectation. There was a widespread resurgence of prayer which had "World-wide Revival" as its specific objective. A great many prayer groups, both on the new mission fields and at home, joined in the intercession, and world-wide links were made. This prayer movement was undoubtedly a fundamental cause of the great awakenings of the first decade of the twentieth century. It is important to notice that these awakenings were not confined to the borders of Wales, but were to be found in very many parts of the world. Revival praying and world impact were intimately linked.

Revival and the missionary call

The pages of Acts have something more to tell us about the connection between the outpouring of the Spirit and world-wide mission. Prayer for revival does not simply stimulate world vision and renew interest in Jesus' world-wide directive for the Church. It also invariably results in many people receiving a specific calling from God to give themselves to missionary outreach. Thus the renewed sense of direction is actually translated into practical and definite action. Vision for the world does not always constitute a call to go and do the work. It is the call from God which has been at the bottom of the work that has actually been done in different parts of the world. While we need to recognise that it does not take a revival to give someone a missionary call, we need equally to see that those times when such calls are few are the times when the Church must pray for a fresh move of the Spirit, so that the calls may be more numerous and more energised.

In Acts we see this happening frequently, and undoubtedly the most obvious example is that of Paul (Acts 9:1ff). Paul's conversion and his subsequent call to "go to the Gentiles" must stand out as one of the most significant effects of the ongoing flood of Holy Spirit activity in the early Church. Desperately trying to stem that flood and battling with his own burdened conscience, Paul was finally converted some two or three years after the initial Pentecostal outpouring. It was a sign and wonder conversion. He saw the risen Lord as a blinding Light, and he literally heard His voice. He saw a vision and was healed. One wonders if this intransigent Pharisee could have come to Christ in any other way!

In Paul's case the conversion and the life-long call came virtually together. He found that he was not only to accept Jesus as the Messiah of his own people, but was also to proclaim Him as Lord to all men. The call was direct and clear. In the first few moments of his conversion experience he asked Jesus, "What do you want me to do?" Within three days Jesus told him that he was to go to the ends of the earth.

It was a phenomenal change of direction for a convinced Jew of Jews, but for the next thirty years he was not "disobedient to the heavenly vision" and he broke open the Gentile world for his new Master. Jerusalem was not the place for him. When soon after beginning his work for Christ, he wanted to bear witness there, he was firmly told by a heavenly visitor to leave that city for wider fields (Acts 22:17ff). Jerusalem was a needy place, but God wanted Paul to work in Tarsus, Antioch, Corinth, Ephesus and other large Gentile cities – even Rome itself.

The commission Paul received was accompanied by a plentiful supply of necessary dynamic. We need to take careful note of that fact. Ananias, through whom the call seems first to have come, was also charged to lay hands on Paul and to bring him both a healing and the filling of the Spirit (Acts 9:15ff). Paul came out of the house in Straight Street, Damascus, not only knowing God's call on his life but knowing also that the power of the Spirit rested on him to enable him to fulfil it.

We do well to pause and reflect that those early disciples could never have imagined when they prayed for the coming of the Spirit that it would lead ultimately to the conversion of Saul. Neither could those who met at a later stage for prayer (Acts 4:30) have thought that their request for God to heal and do mighty signs would be answered by the securing of such a mighty instrument for the Kingdom. But these prayers were answered, and answered in such a way that the Church was able to implement Christ's directive to witness in all the world. This is what prayer for revival can and does lead to.

Paul was a great "tree of planting", but he was by no means the only one. Barnabas, the Levite from Cyprus, was another. We need to note that he was as definitely called to work among Gentiles as Paul was. When the Holy Spirit spoke to the leaders at Antioch (Acts 13:1ff). His words were: "separate Paul and Barnabas to the work to which I have called *them*". Barnabas was as conscious of the Lord's direction upon his life as Paul was. Indeed, in the first instance, Barnabas was the "senior" missionary. In addition, John Mark evidently also felt a call, and later so did such men as Silas, Timothy and Luke himself. There were, therefore, numerous specific callings to mission.

The Moravian phenomenon

When we come to look at the annals of revival we find an abundance of evidence to indicate that this pattern in Acts of powerful mission calls flowing from an outpouring of the Spirit has been repeated very frequently. It would be appropriate to turn to the Moravians here, not merely because they clearly illustrate the point, but also because their emergence as a missionary force flowed directly from revival and, along with the work of Jonathan Edwards, profoundly influenced the growth of modern missions.

As we saw in Chapter 6, the dynamic Christian church which we now know as the Moravians was born effectively in an outpouring of the Spirit in 1727 on a group who had gathered around Count Zinzendorf. That outpouring, the fruit of much prayer by Zinzendorf, moulded together a disunited collection of people of different persuasions into a Spirit-filled community which was full of praise, prayer and love of Jesus. What we need to note for our purposes now, however, is that an extraordinary large number of those people received a direct call to the mission field at a time when the churches in Europe showed virtually no interest in such work, and when those who were interested in it were usually thought of as fanatics.

There is no doubt that Zinzendorf's own prayer and vision had much to do with this. Even as a boy he had a heart for foreign missions. He received it by listening to a handful of men associated with the pietist Franke, men who moved in the Spirit and were active missionaries. At the age of fifteen he made a solemn covenant with a friend to give his life to missions. Mission, therefore, was a burden which was always on his heart. His prayer, vision and commitment came to fruition some twelve years later when, having given refuge to the different religious groups who came to him, he saw the Holy Spirit fall upon them and begin to work in them. One after another they found themselves receiving distinct callings to different parts of the world. Some of those callings actually came before the "great outpouring", but it was that outpouring which provided the all-important dynamic. J. E. Hutton, the Moravian historian, writes:

> It is simply amazing how events turned out. At the time [of going to Zinzendorf's estate] not one of these men had the least idea of becoming a foreign missionary. For that task no men could be better fitted. Each had the blood of martyrs in his veins; each had learned to suffer for his faith. Some had been chilled to the neck in wells: some had been yoked with oxen to the plough.

By 1728 twenty-six young men were ready to go and were giving themselves to arduous training. It was an unparalleled phenomenon in that period. They were the vanguard of a very large missionary force which during the course of the eighteenth century penetrated Greenland, the West Indies, Labrador and the North American Indians. These missionaries, setting out from their base at Herrnhutt and supported by one of the most powerful and persistent prayer chains ever known, became the forerunners and, in many cases, the inspiration of the great wave of missionaries which was to spread all over the world in the nineteenth century. It was not just where these men and their families went that gave the inspiration. It was the spirit in which they went. Wesley was amazed at the clarity of their grasp of the love and salvation of Jesus, and was deeply challenged by their fearlessness in propagating the Gospel. Carey and his friends expressed wonder at "what these Moravians have done". It all originated in revival.

A continuous stream

This stream of specific missionary calls which was so evident among the Moravians has been seen again and again where the Spirit has been outpoured. Some of the greatest figures in the missionary history of the nineteenth century, such as Adoniram Judson, Mary Slessor, Alexander MacKay and James Chalmers, were converted during revivals. Others, like Hudson Taylor, found tremendous invigoration and new vision through revival. Orr reminds us that one of the greatest preachers of the 1859 revival, H. Grattan Guinness, carried his evangelistic passion into foreign missionary work: "in his day Guinness not only won thousands of converts in the revival, but trained more than 1,300 eager volunteers for missionary service". This far-seeing man founded a missionary training college in the wake of the revival.

What was true of the eighteenth and nineteenth centuries has also been true of our own century. The career of R. B. Jones, one of the foremost leaders of the 1904 Welsh Revival, provides us with a fascinating testimony of the link between revival and mission. He recalled how in the midst of all his revival preaching and ministry the matter of world evangelisation became a burden on his heart. It weighed so heavily upon him that he offered himself to the Lord for missionary work. God did not in fact release him to go, but "in all his daily meetings for a long period the missionary challenge was set before the young people who sought to know the yielded, Spirit-filled life". In his book, *Rent Heavens*, he relates how "hundreds of names" during that time were handed to him, "a register of which was carefully kept and for which he prayed". He went on to list some of the very many missionaries who to his knowledge came out of the Welsh Revival. He was not the only person so effected by the Welsh Revival, and speaking of it in general, he finally had this to say "The records of all the missionary societies could bear eloquent testimony to the practical lasting result of the Spirit's work in those days."

Throughout this century revivals have continued to

produce missionaries. It has seen native Solomon Islanders missionising surrounding tribes, Brazilians forming a mission to Europe and the great world-wide Pentecostal explosion flooding many nations with a new phase of missionary expansion. Right up to our own day outpourings of the Spirit have been a major precursor of world evangelisation.

There can be no more important lesson to learn about the nature of revival outpourings than this. Revival is never simply a remedy for the spiritual problems that an individual might face in his own particular area. Revival may help solve those problems, but it is part of something much greater. It is the great means whereby the ultimate purpose of God — that is, to bring blessing throughout the world — is to be fulfilled. Seasons of refreshing are promised until Jesus comes again, and such seasons must come if the great condition for His coming is to be fulfilled. That great condition is that the Gospel should be preached in all the earth and that great harvests should be reaped among all nations. Both of those objectives will be fulfilled only by revival outpourings. When we pray for revival, therefore, we pray for God's ultimate, world-wide purposes and for the coming of the King. This, and nothing less than this, must be our vision.

God has not ordained that in a Christian country there should be an overwhelming mass of foul, helpless poverty.

Lord Shaftesbury

True godliness does not turn men out of the world, but enables them to live in it, and excites their endeavours to mend it.

William Penn

Finney turns out to be an evangelist with a burning social passion, arguing that the spiritual vitality of the church is sapped not by her involvement in social reform but by her avoidance of such issues.

Donald Dayton on Charles Finney

Therefore, as we have opportunity, let us do good to all people.

Galatians 6:10

Chapter 15: People of Love

From time to time those who owned lands or houses sold them, brought the money from the sales . . . and it was distributed to anyone who had need.

Acts 4:34−35

The Spirit who cares

We have seen that when the disciples received the Spirit at Pentecost they found that they began to burn with a great desire to witness to the risen Jesus. That was not the only surge of desire that the Spirit released within them. There arose in their hearts a deep feeling of love. This love was expressed in two directions − first towards God and Jesus, and secondly towards each other. Their love for God manifested itself in glorious outbursts of praise (Acts 2:11, 47), and their love towards each other manifested itself in compassion and practical care. The praise and worship associated with revival is, of course, one of its most beautiful features, but our concern here is with compassion and practical care.

Acts does not say in as many words that the disciples "loved each other". It simply stresses a feature of the life of the early Church which exhibited mutual love *par excellence*, namely the giving away of personal possessions. Luke relates that from the start the believers held everything in common, sold possessions and gave to anyone in need (Acts 2:44−45; 4:32ff). The full significance of this becomes apparent in the light of these words of Jesus: "where your treasure is, there your heart will be also" (Matthew 6:21). The treasure of these disciples found its way into the pockets of those in need, and there is no doubt that such treasure

253

was following the sincere concern of their hearts. The Spirit had touched them deeply with compassion and awareness of others' needs, and they were responding. There was real love abroad.

This sharing of goods was quite clearly not a highly organised push for mutual help instigated by the apostles. It was a purely spontaneous outburst among the believers. There was no apostolic compulsion to hold things in common or to sell land and houses. Those who did not sell things were not ostracised. No "community doctrine" had been developed, and personal property and ownership were never infringed at any point. This giving of money was an expression of the genuine bonding in love which was part of the outpouring of the Spirit. The believers recognised that they were one family and one Body, not simply out of obedience to orthodox exhortation but as a result of a deep, inner, personal Spirit-baptism which taught them that this was the way to live.

It seems to me that the early Church was experiencing something very close to what Paul was describing when he wrote, "we are baptised in one Spirit into one Body" (1 Corinthians 12:13). By this he meant a very great deal more than a mere initiation into the Church. It was a *"baptism in the Spirit into one Body"* that Paul was speaking of. Baptism in the Spirit brings us into one Body, and not simply in a legal and doctrinal sense. It makes us deeply conscious of the fact that we have become part of a Body, that we have real responsibility for that Body, and that we want to embrace that responsibility. It is only the Spirit flowing in us that can actually create this sense of belonging and responsibility and loving. That is why it takes a baptism in the Spirit to turn a cold, formalised church congregation into a living unity. The outpouring of the Spirit at Herrnhutt which the Moravians experienced is a precise example of this. It welded a disunited group into a powerful, loving fellowship.

Whatever the precise implications of Paul's statement might be, the fact remains that the Church of the Book of

Acts was full of love and care, and that the unity it experienced was a work of the Spirit. Widows were regularly fed (6:1) and the poor were always kept in mind (11:29). In other words, the stream of the Spirit produced a social awareness alongside a spiritual awareness. The Spirit who energised for evangelism also energised for practical and social care. This will always be a characteristic of genuine revival.

From Dorcas to Wesley

The record in Acts shows us that while in the early Church such activity went on largely amongst the Christian believers, it also reached a far wider sphere. One obvious pointer is to be found in the humble yet much-acknowledged work of Dorcas (Acts 6:36). Luke tells us that "she was always doing good and helping the poor", and that she gave a great deal of her time to making clothes for widows. Here was love pouring out "to all men". This, of course, does not amount to a picture of widespread social reform! But it does underline the principle on which such activity is built, namely that the love of God was never intended to stop at the boundaries of the Church but was meant to find a natural extension outside it. Moreover, such personal and dedicated concern to meet a perceived need is really the only seed from which wider and grander social activity can grow. If revivals show us anything they show us that again and again it is through converted and socially dedicated individuals that powerful works for the general well-being of people have come into being.

What we need to observe, therefore, about the outpouring of the Spirit at Pentecost is that it brought with it the dynamic for widespread practical action to relieve the distress and meet the needs of others. An outpouring of the Spirit will always recharge the batteries of social concern. When the Church is indifferent or impotent in the areas of general human need it desperately needs such a recharge.

It may seem a very big jump from such a humble woman

255

as Dorcas to evangelistic giants of the stature of Paul and Whitefield. But the Spirit of love who worked through Dorcas also worked in a very similar fashion in both these men. Paul had a very deep interest in the poor and was constantly involved in their relief. He was responsible for the delivery of aid from Antioch to Jerusalem (Acts 11:30), and his missionary journeys saw him systematically collecting and administering financial help for the poor (2 Corinthians 8 and 9). This was practical social concern on a wider, more impressive scale, but the dynamic was the same.

Whitefield's ministry demonstrates a similar concern. Very shortly after his ordination and his immediate success as a preacher he was back in Oxford, involved in work which he described in his Journal in these words:

> During this time I was given charge over the donations for the poor prisoners . . . two or three charity schools were also under my care . . . I enjoyed distributing money and books among the poor prisoners and employing as many as could work. By this they were kept from the worst of jail diseases . . . idleness.

This practical social activity never ceased throughout the whole of his ministry. Great evangelist that he was, he always remembered the needs of the poor. It was a constant custom of Whitefield's to take collections after the meetings he addressed. The beneficiaries of such collections were many and various, as the following extracts from his Journal show:

> I preached and collected for the needs of the poor prisoners in Newgate two to three times a week.

> It was my practice to nourish my acquaintance with the rich for the benefit of the poor. I recommended two poor clergymen to their [some rich ladies'] charity. They said little but . . . gave about thirty-six guineas.

People gave so liberally to the charity schools that nearly one thousand pounds sterling was collected at several churches.

The orphan boys and girls looked on me as their great benefactor.

He brushed aside envious accusations that he was a spiritual pickpocket. They did not prevent him from actually standing with the collection box in his own hand after he had finished preaching. It was not his calling, of course, to run the orphanages and charity schools himself, but he was an enormous encouragement and provider for those who did. He epitomised the spirit of revival: he recharged social concern.

One might have chosen almost identical quotations for John Wesley. Indeed, with Wesley it is possible to see this same spirit of practical social care taking an even more strategic direction. John Stott says of this great eighteenth-century evangelist: "Wesley was both a preacher and a prophet of social righteousness." These are not words we are normally accustomed to hear of Wesley, but they are true and they bring to the fore a vital part of his great revival ministry. His work had an enormous impact socially. This great proclaimer of the "New Birth" was also the author of a book about the slave trade called *Thoughts upon Slavery*. In it he totally denounced that inhuman traffic, so unthinkingly accepted by the vast majority of his contemporaries. He exposed both the greed and hypocrisy that lay behind it, and showed the way in which it bred other evils. He attacked the wealthy slave merchants very sharply and described those who worked for them as kidnappers and murderers. Edwin Orr comments, "These were strong words to use freely in 1774, when slaving itself was protected by law, when philosophers of old and statesmen of the time were quoted to justify the outrageous institution."

Even political involvement!

Wesley was not just a declaimer through the written word. He had a personal link with William Wilberforce in Parliament, and even on his deathbed he wrote to encourage him to pursue his political endeavours to get the slave trade abolished. The political processes, therefore, were no stumbling block to John Wesley. Righteousness must be fought for, and sometimes it was necessary to do battle in the political arena. Without any question, he recognised the calling and responsibility that rested on the shoulders of Wilberforce and, though no politician himself, he was determined to be in his own way a strength to his fellow worker for Christ.

Wilberforce was, of course, one of a powerful group of able and persistent men who had been deeply influenced by the eighteenth-century Evangelical Revival and in particular by that part of it which affected the Anglican Church. Such revivals produce not isolated individuals with a heart for social activity but significant groups of like-minded people. Almost all those who spoke out for the abolition of slavery and then engineered its passage through Parliament were products of the Evangelical Revival.

However, successful legislative activity does not depend entirely upon prominent, God-given figures. Social and moral improvement at a national level depends upon a general quickening of social conscience. Unrighteous vested interests only fall when exposed to a widespread awakened moral rejection of evil. It is precisely that awakened moral note which revival frequently supplies. This seems to have been the outcome of the great preaching campaigns of Wesley and Whitefield in the eighteenth century. The major legislative social gains made in the nineteenth century were achieved against the background of powerful spiritual movements.

There is a great difference between Dorcas' ministry in a Palestinian village and Wilberforce's crusade against slavery at Westminster. But behind both expressions of social concern was the same dynamic — that is, the sense of compassionate obligation towards humanity that a true outpouring of the Spirit leaves upon the Church.

It would be easy to catalogue a vast list of agencies which have sprung up out of personal concern for those in need and which have their roots in spiritual revival. Many such agencies have provided models for national legislation, especially in education, hospitals, orphanages, rescue homes, prison reform and the like. It was revival movements which gave the agencies their inspiration and impetus. When the Spirit flows such work always follows. Suffice it to say that revival means a release of concern and practical activity amongst the needy, which may be expressed in personal, institutional or political ways. Injustice, poverty, oppression, pain and suffering are not ignored by the Spirit of God. Neither are they ignored by the Church through which He flows in power.

Praying for revival means praying, perhaps with repentance, for that kind of flow of the Spirit that restores to the Body of Christ the boldness and vision and the compassion and zeal to take every initiative for the restoration of righteousness and peace. Some may not feel inclined to agree with all that Finney had to say about revival, but there is no mistaking the deep social concern that led him to pen the following words:

Now the great business of the church is to reform the world — to put away every kind of sin. The Christian church was designed to make aggressive movements in every direction — to lift her voice and put forth her energies against iniquity in high and low places — to reform individuals, communities and governments, until every form of iniquity is driven from the earth.

He was a great evangelist, and many of the greatest evangelists the world has seen have felt the same compulsion of spirit. This was what made them true men of revival.

The modern world is not shorn of opportunities for social and practical care. Opportunities are abundant. If prayer for revival results in a major resurgence of vision and the calling out of Christians to pick up more and more of those opportunities, that alone will make that prayer immensely worthwhile.

Epilogue: Moving with the Vision

One of the interesting facts that emerges from a look at history is that the final decades of both the eighteenth and nineteenth centuries were marked by powerful and widespread prayer movements. They were movements in which there was a specific calling on God for an outpouring of the Spirit. The word "revival" was unashamedly used to describe the desire that was in the hearts of those who were involved.

The eighteenth-century prayer movement brought about a mighty surge of the Spirit which, as we have seen, not only affected Britain and America but also initiated powerful evangelisation in hitherto unreached areas of the world. The momentum continued, even increased, during the nineteenth century. The prayer movement of the final decade of that century was world-wide in scope and, as the twentieth century got under way, resulted in outpourings of the Spirit which were themselves world-wide. As with the previous century, the momentum has continued and vast numbers of people all over the world have come to Christ.

We have now come once again to the final decade of a century. One of the most exciting things we can detect is a growing heart-feeling among very many Christians that we should be seeking God for an outpouring of the Spirit. This is not happening simply because people are trying to repeat history. That would be quite disastrous, for though history does repeat itself it can hardly be made to do so! It is happening spontaneously and, very significantly, it is happening all over the western world. There is an increasing seeking and an increasing expectancy. I think nothing could be more significant for the dawn of the twenty-first century.

Some have felt that the word "revival" is a little obsolete, a pointer to old historical monuments. It all depends, of course, on the connotation one gives to a word. I would not be averse to the word being replaced if a better one could be found. It would undoubtedly be tragic if the essential truth which the word enshrines — namely, the release of the Holy Spirit in great and powerful waves in answer to prayer — were to be thought obsolete. Woe betide the Church if it makes the testimony of Acts obsolete. Dryness and fleshly activity alone would then remain.

It is a fine thing to conceive of the last years of our century as a decade of evangelism. But it is a decade which really calls for something deeper than that. It is a decade which is calling for the re-establishment in the Church of a new dynamic by the Holy Spirit. The cry for the Spirit must precede the committee planning. We need to call on God to act in the way that only He can. Earnest, widespread prayer to God specifically for the outpouring of the Spirit will see the release of evangelism of a kind that no amount of dutiful programming can ever produce. History vouches for that.

The cry for revival (or whatever else it may be called) must get back into the bloodstream of the Church in the next ten years. There may well be some very large gatherings of Christians for the purpose of prayer, but the work will be done in great measure by small groups of ministers and leaders meeting together regularly to seek God for a work of the Spirit. And it will be done by groups of Christian people, both within and across the denominational divides, following the example of their leaders (or, as so frequently happens, giving the leaders an example). Monthly and quarterly prayer rallies need to proliferate. It is fascinating to see the emergence of very many early morning prayer sessions of this kind. Perhaps they will be a key feature of the years that lie ahead. The early morning has a freshness and a fragrance (once we are awake!) that gives such prayer great impetus.

The stuff of praying for revival has been outlined in this book. Revival involves every aspect of what might be called the "Spirit-drenched Church" — it entails powerful baptisms in the Spirit, widespread conviction of sin, large gatherings and reapings of the unconverted, anointed preachers and evangelists, a loving impact on society. There is room for earnest prayer in many areas. We particularly need to pray over those areas for which our hearts have been given a special burden.

If history has anything to teach us, it is simply this: where there has been a stirring of God's people and a laying hold of revival vision in prayer, there has always been a quickening in the Church. That is the challenge we need to respond to in the decade before us. The challenge is not to pray for prayer's sake but to seek an answer from heaven. We must go into the next century with the winds of God blowing across the Western world as powerfully as they have blown across other parts of the globe during this century. Nothing less will suffice.